CONTENTS

HOW TO USE THIS BOOK

General Capabilities form one dimension of the Australian Curriculum, the others being the Learning Areas and the Cross-Curriculum Priorities. General Capabilities are taught through the content of the Learning Areas and involve knowledge, skills, behaviour and dispositions.

There are seven General Capabilities, and this Targeting General Capabilities book examines two of them: Personal and Social Capability, and Intercultural Understanding. The two General Capabilities are further divided into their elements: seven in all. Each unit begins with a stimulus, followed by assessable activities that examine the element through the different Learning Areas. The table below provides a quick page reference to the different Learning Areas examined via each General Capability element in this book. You will find the relevant links to the Australian Curriculum at the beginning of each section.

Unit	Elements	English	HASS	HPE	Maths	Science	Tech	The Arts
	Personal & Social Capability							
1	Self- awareness	6		8	10	12		14
2	Self-management	17, 19	21	25			23	
3	Social awareness	28, 30	32, 34	36				
4	Social management	39	41		43		47	
	Intercultural Understanding							
5	Recognising culture	59	61, 63	67			65	
6	Interacting & empathising	70	72, 74					76, 78
7	Reflecting & taking responsibility	81	83, 85	89	87			

On the last page of each unit, space is allocated for self-reflection. Students have the opportunity to explore what they have learnt about each element and to record their thoughts.

There is an assessment section at the end of each General Capability element where tasks are tailored to the sub-elements, rather than through the lens of a specific Learning Area. This consolidates students' understanding of the concepts and provides guidance for further reflection.

Personal & Social Capability

Personal and Social Capability encourage children to be aware of their emotions and learn how to manage their feelings, behaviours and interactions with others. As outlined in the curriculum, the elements and sub-elements are:

 **Self-awareness** — recognise emotions; recognise personal qualities and achievements; understand themselves as learners; develop reflective practice

 **Self-management** — express emotions appropriately; develop self-discipline and set goals; work independently and show initiative; become confident, resilient and adaptable

 **Social awareness** — appreciate diverse perspectives; contribute to civil society; understand relationships

 **Social management** — communicate effectively; work collaboratively; make decisions, negotiate and resolve conflict; develop leadership skills.

Self-awareness

How do you get to school each day? The Pedestrian Council of Australia recommends walking for its health benefits, and it encourages families to walk to school instead of driving. For more than 20 years, they have promoted the annual 'Walk Safely to School Day'. You've probably seen the advertisements on television, and you may have noticed (and even coloured in) posters like this one:

ACTIVE KIDS ARE SMARTER KIDS

WALK PLENTY IN 2020

WALK PLENTY IN 2020

WALK SAFELY TO SCHOOL DAY

FRIDAY 11 SEPTEMBER 2020

Until they're ten, children must always hold an adult's hand when crossing the road

WALK.COM.AU

@nationalwalksafelytoschoolday @natwalktoschool @natwalktoschool #WSTSD

SUPPORTED BY THE AUSTRALIAN GOVERNMENT AND ALL STATE, TERRITORY AND LOCAL GOVERNMENTS

TARGETING GENERAL CAPABILITIES YEARS 3-4 © PASCAL PRESS ISBN: 9781925726220

The Pedestrian Council says that the aims of 'Walk Safely to School Day' are to:

- promote the health benefits of walking
- encourage parents and carers to walk young children to school
- make sure that children under eight hold an adult's hand on the footpath, in carparks, and while crossing the road
- make sure that children aged up to ten are supervised and hold an adult's hand while crossing the road
- help children develop road-crossing skills
- reduce air pollution and traffic congestion caused by cars.

If you don't already walk to school, maybe you can discuss it with your family. Walking is free, it doesn't cause pollution, and it's good for you!

Getting off the bus on the way to school can be dangerous. The Pedestrian Council tells us to Stop! Look! Listen! Think! Stop one step back from the kerb. Look both ways. Listen for traffic and think about whether it's safe to cross. Be sure to always choose a safe place to cross the road, such as at traffic lights or a pedestrian crossing.

English – Literacy

Australian Curriculum Links: *ACELY1678, ACELY1680, ACELY1691, ACELY1692*

Some people walk to school and back, some use public transport and others are driven in cars. It might not seem like a big deal, but the choices you and your family make can have a huge impact on the environment, your health and wellbeing, and even your marks in class!

Look at the poster on page 4 and answer the following questions.

Who is the 'Walk Safely to School Day' poster aimed at?

a) doctors and nurses

b) train and bus drivers

c) parents and children

d) the Pedestrian Council of Australia

How would you describe the appearance of the poster?

a) bright and colourful

b) gloomy and dark

c) factual and plain

d) threatening and scary

How do you think the children in the poster are feeling?

a) frightened of crossing the road

b) cross at being made to walk to school

c) happy and safe because they are holding hands

d) happy that they are getting a day off school

TARGETING GENERAL CAPABILITIES YEARS 3-4 © PASCAL PRESS ISBN: 9781925726220

Self-awareness

4 The slogan 'Walk plenty in 2020' is an example of ...

a) alliteration. b) rhyme. c) onomatopoeia. d) assonance.

5 The poster ...

a) provides information.

b) encourages a course of action.

c) identifies how you can find out more.

d) all of the above.

6 What do you think is meant by the poster heading 'Active kids are smarter kids'?

____

____

7 Some people live too far from school to walk all the way. Suggest ways in which they can still take part in 'Walk Safely to School Day'.

____

____

Your view

8 What are your attitudes to walking to school? List some positive and some negative points in the table below, then come to a conclusion.

Positives	Negatives

I think that, for me, walking to school is a (circle one choice) good / bad idea because

____

____

Health & Physical Education

Australian Curriculum Links: *ACPPS035, ACPPS036*

Walking to school—all or at least some of the way—is a great way to get more active, but busy roads are dangerous, and everyone needs to learn how to stay safe when out and about. The Pedestrian Council's cartoon below shows some of the challenges young children face.

Friday 11 September 2020

Until they're ten, children must always hold an adult's hand when crossing the road

Examine the cartoon then answer the following questions.

 **Young children are good at judging the speed of oncoming cars.**

True False

 **It can be hard for drivers to see small children, especially if they come out from between parked cars.**

True False

 **Children can't always work out which direction a sound is coming from.**

True False

 **Children are highly focused on road safety and cannot be distracted.**

True False

 **Do you think it is a good idea to run when crossing the road? Why or why not?**

____

____

TARGETING GENERAL CAPABILITIES YEARS 3-4 © PASCAL PRESS ISBN: 9781925726220

6 Examine the map below. Find and name two busy roads.

Hint: The wider a road appears on the map, the busier it is.

____

7 Vasudha and her mother have decided to walk to school every day. Can you help them trace a safe path?

Hint: Vasudha should stay on footpaths and cross busy roads at traffic lights and pedestrian crossings.

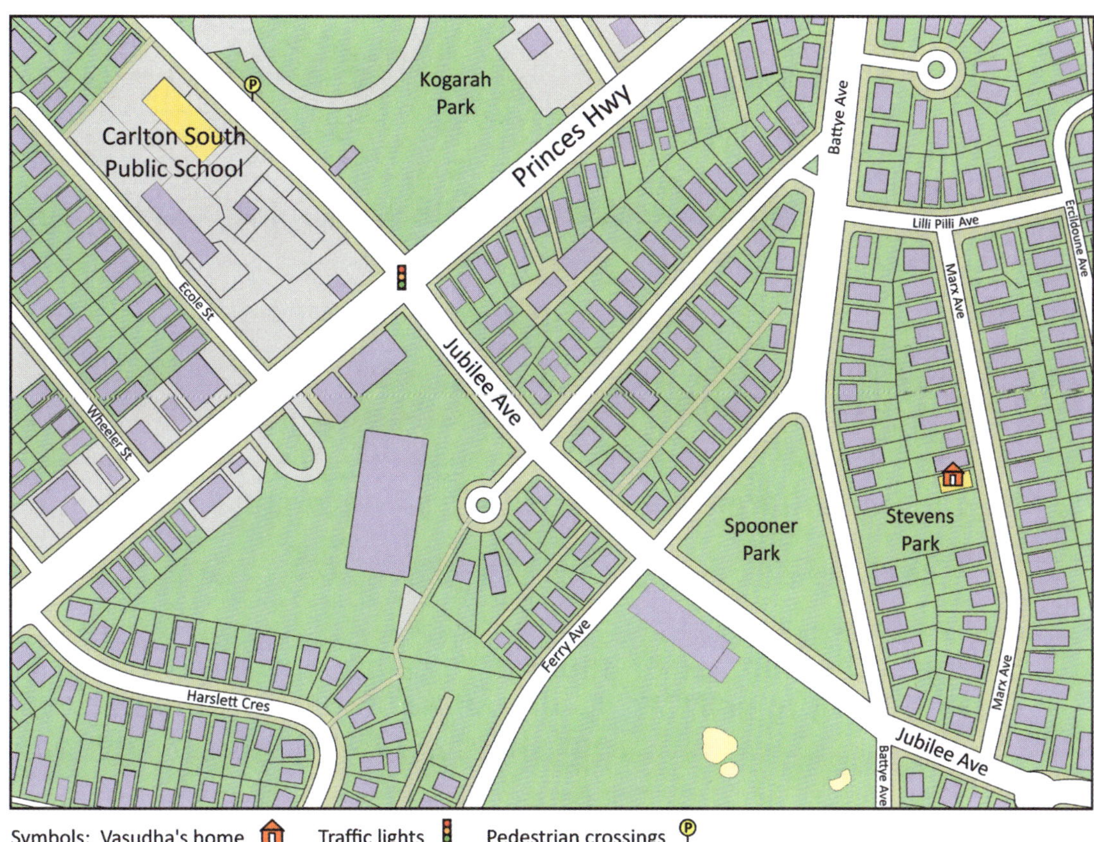

Symbols: Vasudha's home   Traffic lights   Pedestrian crossings

8 This is what I have learnt about staying safe on the roads when I go for a walk:

____

____

____

____

Mathematics – Number and Algebra

Australian Curriculum Links: *ACMNA058, ACMNA077*

After deciding to walk to school each day, Vasudha wanted to know how the children in her dance class travelled to school. She asked and got the following answers:

Walk	4 (including herself)
Car	1
Bus	3
Train	2

We can understand this information better if we use fractions. A fraction is a part of a whole. Fractions are written like this:1/2. The number on top of the line is the numerator, and it tells us how many parts we have. The number on the bottom is the denominator, and it tells us how many parts the whole was divided into. The fraction 1/2 means that a whole has been divided into 2 parts, and we have 1 part of that whole—that is, one half.

Answer the following questions.

How many children are in Vasudha's dance class (the 'whole')?

____

Shade in the number of squares to represent the children that catch a train to school.

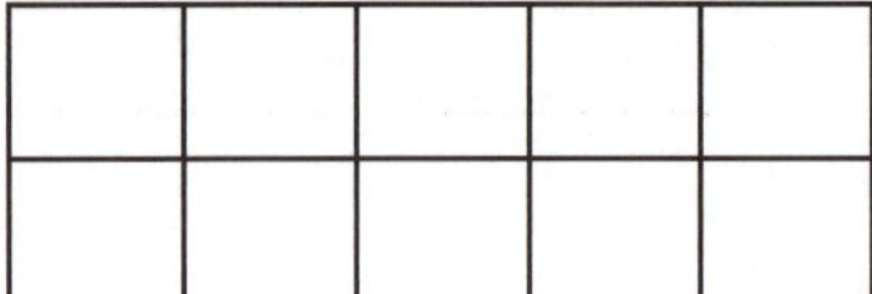

What part of the class catches a train? Express your answer as a fraction.

____

What part of the class walks to school? Express your answer as a fraction.

____

TARGETING GENERAL CAPABILITIES YEARS 3-4 © PASCAL PRESS ISBN: 9781925726220

Equivalent fractions are different fractions that are really the same number. The chart below divides up a whole in different ways—into halves, thirds, quarters and so on up to tenths—like a strip of paper that's been folded up in different ways.

Look at the equivalent fractions chart below, then answer the questions.

one whole									
1/2	1/2								
1/3	1/3	1/3							
1/4	1/4	1/4	1/4						
1/5	1/5	1/5	1/5	1/5					
1/8	1/8	1/8	1/8	1/8	1/8	1/8	1/8		
1/10	1/10	1/10	1/10	1/10	1/10	1/10	1/10	1/10	1/10

What fraction can 2/10 also be expressed as?

____

What fraction can 2/8 also be expressed as?

____

Which fraction is bigger, 2/8 or 2/10?

____

Which fraction is smaller, 3/10 or 1/5?

____

PERSONAL & SOCIAL CAPABILITY

Science

Australian Curriculum Links: *ACSSU076, ACHSHE051, ACSHEO62*

Friction is a type of force. It's caused when two objects move or rub against each other. Think about when you rub your hands together on a cold winter's day. That warmth you feel is caused by friction.

Friction is what allows us to walk. We push our feet against the ground. Thanks to friction, our feet grip the ground and we move forwards. If there was little or no friction,—like on an ice rink—our feet wouldn't get a good grip and they'd slide out from underneath us. That's why it's easier to walk on a rough, textured path than it is on slippery wet grass.

Similarly, if the soles of our shoes are smooth, they rub less against the ground than if we wear shoes with ridged, gripping soles. We'd be more likely to slip and fall, especially on a smooth or wet floor.

The same principles apply to cars on the road. In wet weather, when the road is slippery, there's less friction between the road and the tyres. This makes it harder for cars to stop. They'll travel a lot further than they would if the road was dry. Keep this in mind if you walk to school on a rainy day!

Read the information above and answer the following questions.

The warmth you feel when you rub your hands together is caused by ...

a) static electricity.

b) magnetism.

c) friction.

d) all of the above.

What would happen if we tried to walk on a surface with little or no friction?

a) We would walk very slowly.

b) We would be likely to slip and fall.

c) We would walk comfortably and quickly.

d) We would see no difference.

TARGETING GENERAL CAPABILITIES YEARS 3-4 © PASCAL PRESS ISBN: 9781925726220

3 Friction is lower on ...

a) smooth surfaces.
b) rough surfaces.
c) wet surfaces.
d) a and c.

4 Wearing shoes with smooth soles makes it harder for you to slip over.

True False

5 Cars find it harder to slow down and stop on wet days.

True False

6 After braking, cars travel further on wet roads than they do on dry roads.

True False

7 You need to be extra careful if walking to school on wet days.

True False

Your turn

8 You can see friction in action in this simple experiment. You'll need a toy car and a ramp, which you'll set up on a variety of surfaces. Some surfaces should be rough, others smooth. For example, try tiles, floorboards, carpet, fabric and cardboard. Take the car to the top of the ramp and release it, placing a marker to show where the car stopped on each surface. Along which surface did the car go the furthest? Is that what you expected? Explain.

PERSONAL & SOCIAL CAPABILITY

TARGETING GENERAL CAPABILITIES YEARS 3-4 © PASCAL PRESS ISBN: 9781925726220

The Arts – Visual Arts

Australian Curriculum Links: *ACAVAM110, ACAVAM112*

PERSONAL & SOCIAL CAPABILITY

We look at visual symbols to help us understand what something means. Often it's easier to gain information from an image than from words. For example, look at the map on page 9. Symbols identify a house, traffic lights and pedestrian crossings. They were used because they're recognisable, they fit on the map, and they're easy to spot.

Usually symbols look like the thing they represent. For instance, a long line with bars across it represents a railway line, while a group of triangles represents mountains. The symbols are also often coloured to match what they depict: clusters of trees are green, and rivers are blue.

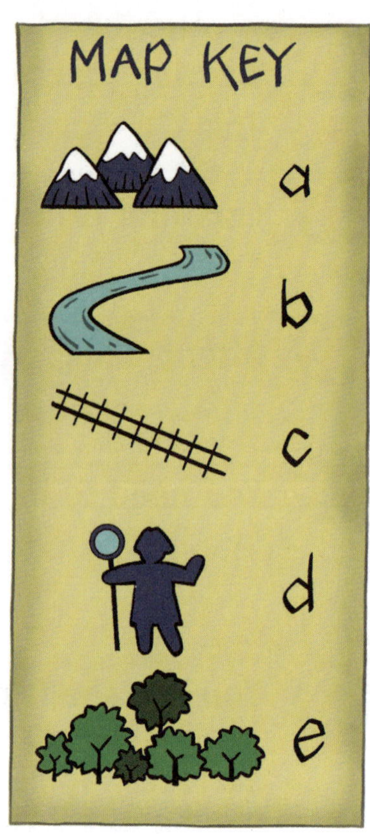

A map's key explains the symbols used on the map. Look at the key and match the symbols in the key to the features they represent.

 **Which symbol represents a mountain?**

____

 **Which symbol represents a train line?**

____

 **Which symbol represents a school?**

____

 **Which symbol represents bushland?**

____

 **Which symbol represents a river?**

____

TARGETING GENERAL CAPABILITIES YEARS 3-4 © PASCAL PRESS ISBN: 9781925726220

Word bank

footpath | swamp | golf course | hospital
footbridge | quarry | cave | police station

6. **Use the word bank to list features you might find in a safe walking environment.**

____

____

7. **Use the word bank to list features you might find in an unsafe walking environment.**

____

____

Your turn

8. **Draw your own key of map symbols for the features listed in the word bank.**

____

____

____

____

Self-reflection

This unit was about self-awareness. What have you learnt about your ability to develop new skills, such as walking safely to school?

____

____

____

____

PERSONAL & SOCIAL CAPABILITY

BENN HARRADINE – THE COLOURFUL SPORTS STAR

You won't read many biographies about successful people who achieved their triumphs without effort. It's far more common to read about their struggles, their dedication and their determination to succeed despite the odds.

This is certainly true for Benn Harradine. Born in 1982, Harradine loved sport from an early age, but when he was only eight, doctors discovered he had a rare liver condition that would prevent him from competing in contact sports. Harradine didn't let this become a dream destroyer, however. Switching to field athletics, he quickly developed an interest in discus throwing—a passion that would take him all the way to the Olympic Games.

Benn Harradine was the first Australian Aboriginal to compete in a field athletics event in the Olympics. Harradine is from the Watjabaluk peoples, but he knew nothing about his background until he turned 22. Enthusiastically embracing his heritage, he became a mentor for Aboriginal athletes. He travelled to Aboriginal communities to teach them track and field skills, and they taught him about their food, dance and culture.

Even so, we can't assume things were always easy for the sports star. Harradine performed well in the 2006 Commonwealth games, but he wasn't so happy with his results in the 2008 Olympics. He found his motivation slipping and knew he had to do something about it. Harradine started wearing vibrantly colourful sports outfits in an attempt to bring back some of the joy (see photo on page 23). It worked! By focusing on giving it his all—without obsessing about the results—he smashed it. He won gold in the 2010 Commonwealth games, and it can be said that his colourful outfits glittered as brightly as his medal!

TARGETING GENERAL CAPABILITIES YEARS 3-4 © PASCAL PRESS ISBN: 9781925726220

English – Literature

Australian Curriculum Links: *ACELT1596, ACELT1603, ACELT1791*

Reading inspirational stories about other people's lives can help us to improve our own. We can learn from how they coped with challenges and obstacles, even if their problems were nothing like ours. Seeing how they persisted when facing defeat helps us to keep going too. Whether their story is about success in sport, music, art or simply coping with life's hardships, we feel encouraged knowing that others have also faced difficulties yet still managed to triumph.

Read the text on page 16 and answer the following questions.

The text is an example of ...

a) a narrative.

b) an exposition.

c) an advertisement.

d) a biography.

'Dream destroyer' is an example of ...

a) onomatopoeia.

b) rhyme.

c) alliteration.

d) spoonerism.

'Smash' is an example of ...

a) onomatopoeia.

b) rhyme.

c) alliteration.

d) spoonerism.

Self-management

4 What is the purpose of the text?

a) to entertain

b) to inform

c) to encourage others

d) all of the above

5 What could another title for the text be?

a) Why You Should Wear Bright Clothes

b) How to Throw a Discus

c) The Importance of Not Giving Up

d) Researching Your Family's Ancestry

Test your general knowledge

6 Benn Harradine won awards for his discus skills. What is a discus?

___

7 Discus throwing was an event in the ancient Olympic Games. Which country did the Olympic Games originate in?

___

Your view

8 Do you recognise any of Benn Harradine's struggles in your own life? Explain.

___

___

___

___

TARGETING GENERAL CAPABILITIES YEARS 3-4 © PASCAL PRESS ISBN: 9781925726220

English – Literacy

Australian Curriculum Links: *ACELY1678, ACELY1679, ACELY1690, ACELY1691*

Informative texts give us information about a person, place or event. Biographies are a type of informative text. They give us an account of someone's life that was written by somebody else. If the person wrote it themselves, it's called an autobiography.

Usually biographies are about famous people. Often, they worked hard to overcome obstacles and meet their goals. Biographies can be short, taking the form of news or magazine articles, web pages or encyclopedia entries. They can also be long, for example chapters of books or even entire books about one person.

Whatever their length or form, biographies often:

- begin with something interesting to gain the reader's attention
- introduce the reason the biography was written
- use paragraphs, headings and/or chapters to separate events
- use the third person
- use the past tense
- have a conclusion that makes the reader think about the person's life and influence.

Read the text on page 16 and answer the following questions.

The text is an informative text.

True False

The text is most likely an autobiography.

True False

The text is likely to have been written for a magazine or website.

True False

4 The text is written in the ...

a) first person.

b) second person.

c) third person.

d) all of the above

5 The text is written in the ...

a) past tense.

b) present tense.

c) future tense.

d) all of the above

6 What is the biographer's opinion of Benn Harradine?

a) He is someone to be pitied.

b) He is resilient and strong.

c) He is a talented athlete.

d) b and c

7 Find some key words or phrases in the text that show the biographer's attitude to Harradine.

____

____

Your view

8 Do you think that the biographer succeeded in writing an inspirational story? Why or why not?

____

____

TARGETING GENERAL CAPABILITIES YEARS 3-4 © PASCAL PRESS ISBN: 9781925726220

HASS – History

Australian Curriculum Links: *ACHASSK065, ACHASSI052, ACHASSI073*

The Olympic Games celebrate the sports ideal. They celebrate hard work, self-discipline and dedication. Once every four years, nations from around the world come together to take part in the summer Olympics. Athletes have to train very hard to take part, and many consider competing in the Olympics to be the highlight of their careers.

The games are hosted in different locations across the globe. During the opening and closing ceremonies, the host nation has the opportunity to celebrate its history and culture and share these with the world. Australia has competed in every summer Olympics since the first one in 1896 and has hosted them twice: in Melbourne in 1956 and in Sydney in 2000.

The games originated in ancient Greece in 776 BC in the sanctuary of Olympia. Although a sporting event, they were essentially a religious festival in honour of the god Zeus. Greeks from different city states gathered together to compete in peace—and that spirit still applies to the Olympics today.

Even so, there have been challenging times when the modern Olympics have been cancelled or postponed. The games were cancelled in 1916, 1940 and 1944. The 2020 games were postponed due to the outbreak of COVID-19, but—like the resilience and dedication that the games celebrate—the Olympic Games always come back.

Read the text above and answer the following questions.

What do the Olympic Games celebrate?

a) dedication to achieving goals

b) competing with peace and respect

c) blending sport with education and culture

d) all of the above

PERSONAL & SOCIAL CAPABILITY

Self-management

When has Australia hosted the summer Olympics?

a) 1896 and 1956

b) 1956 and 2000

c) 1916 and 1940

d) never

PERSONAL & SOCIAL CAPABILITY

Where did the Olympic Games originate?

a) Olympia

b) Athens

c) Paris

d) Melbourne

The Olympic Games were originally a/an ________________ festival.

a) folk music

b) arts

c) religious

d) comedy

The modern Olympic Games are exactly the same as the ancient ones.

True False

The Olympic Games were cancelled during WWI and WWII.

True False

The 2020 games were postponed because they were too expensive to run.

True False

Your view

Do you think the Olympics should be cancelled or postponed in difficult times? Explain.

____

____

TARGETING GENERAL CAPABILITIES YEARS 3-4 © PASCAL PRESS ISBN: 9781925726220

Technologies – Digital Technologies

Australian Curriculum Link: *ACTDIP013*

GETTY IMAGES

As a champion athlete, Benn Harradine felt he had a responsibility to promote the discus. He wanted to increase awareness of the sport and engage the public, so in 2014 he started a social media campaign. Using the hashtag #willitthrow, he invited people to challenge him to hurl various objects to see how far they would go. Since then he's thrown a startling array of objects, including an avocado, a meat pie, a tin of baked beans, an iPhone and even a humus-filled sock! He developed a large following and succeeded in increasing awareness of the discus in a playful and fun way.

Sharing things through social media can be a good way to provide information or to draw attention to various causes—but it also carries many risks ...

Ming is a wonderful dancer, and her best friend Gina videoed her on a smartphone. Without asking permission, Gina shared the video on social media. The video was filmed in the school hall, and the school crest was visible in the background. Gina identified Ming by name.

Think about the problems this can cause, then answer the following questions.

Sharing the video on social media was an invasion of Ming's ...

a) privacy.

b) home.

c) friendship.

d) safety.

Self-management

2 What should Gina have done before sharing the video?

a) asked for permission

b) made sure the school crest was not visible

c) been careful not to include Ming's name

d) all of the above

3 As a general rule, who should you share content with?

a) friends and other trusted acquaintances

b) family

c) the general public

d) a and b only

4 By identifying Ming and the school, Gina was putting her friend in danger from strangers.

True False

5 Strangers may hide their identity online and pretend to be someone that they are not.

True False

6 Content that is shared on social media can easily be deleted.

True False

7 Some people made nasty comments about Ming's dancing and she was very upset. What can Gina do about these comments?

____

____

Your view

8 Write examples of the type of content you would think twice about before sharing.

____

____

____

TARGETING GENERAL CAPABILITIES YEARS 3-4 © PASCAL PRESS ISBN: 9781925726220

Health & Physical Education

Australian Curriculum Links: *ACPPS033, ACPPS036*

Our successes, challenges and even our failures all help to make us stronger. They help us to learn more about ourselves by finding out our strengths and weaknesses. Knowing what works and what doesn't can guide us when faced with unfamiliar situations in the future. This is true for all sorts of challenges in life—whether we are trying to get better at something (such as sport or schoolwork) or dealing with difficult life situations (such as moving home or changing schools).

Read the text on page 16 and answer the following questions.

1. **What setback did Benn Harradine face when he was eight years old?**

   ____

   ____

2. **What did he do to overcome this problem?**

   ____

   ____

3. **Why did Benn Harradine's motivation start to slip after he competed in the 2008 Olympic Games?**

   ____

   ____

4. **What does the text say Benn Harradine did to help him gain back his motivation? Did it work? Why?**

   ____

   ____

   ____

   ____

PERSONAL & SOCIAL CAPABILITY

Self-management

Use one of the words below to help you fill in the missing words in the cloze passages below.

optimists succeed family early

 Wearing colourful clothes helped motivate Benn Harradine. He also tried other strategies, such as finding a new coach. There are many things that can support us in hard times, such as getting help from friends and ________________.

 Attitude is important. Pessimists believe that things will turn out badly. ____________, on the other hand, believe things will turn out well.

 If you have a problem, it's a good idea to seek help ___________, rather than leaving it for later when the problem might become harder to solve.

 Persisting in a task means not giving up. It may be hard at first, but if you don't give up, you are more likely to _______________ in the end.

PERSONAL & SOCIAL CAPABILITY

Self-reflection

This unit was about self-management. What have you learnt about your ability to keep going when facing difficult challenges?

____

____

TARGETING GENERAL CAPABILITIES YEARS 3-4 © PASCAL PRESS ISBN: 9781925726220

CALLS FOR NEW ROAD AS RESIDENTS RECOVER FROM SAVAGE FIRE SEASON

Calls have been made to build a new highway through the scenic Snowy Monaro region. This comes following the 2020 bushfire season, which hit with a ferocity that took the nation by surprise.

'The Monaro Highway was cut by fire,' says Alice Schwartz, president of the newly formed Monaro Residents' Association. 'We were lucky to get out before the road closed.'

Not everybody was so fortunate. Some residents who wanted to flee had no choice but to shelter in their homes. They faced a frightening time as thousands of hectares were burnt by the devastating fires. Although several homes were destroyed, thankfully no residents lost their lives.

'Who knows what might happen next time?' Schwartz says. 'We need another way out, before lives are lost. We need a new four-lane highway with quicker access to safety zones.'

However, not everybody agrees with her. The proposed new highway cuts through a Declared Aboriginal Place. The spiritual home of the Ngarigo people, the elders say that a new road would destroy the area, which is rich with cultural significance. They would like to see the road redirected, to prevent damage to the sacred site.

The Monaro Residents' Association is willing to work with the Ngarigo people to find an alternative location, but Bill Thomas, a local environmental activist, is against any new roadwork.

'It's totally unnecessary,' Thomas insists. 'The problem isn't roads—we have enough roads. The problem is climate change. We need to stop global warming to lessen the bushfires. How can causing more damage to the environment make things better?'

TARGETING GENERAL CAPABILITIES YEARS 3-4 © PASCAL PRESS ISBN: 9781925726220

English – Language

Australian Curriculum Links: *ACELA1477, ACELA1488*

There are many different views in a society, and people don't always agree with each other. In the news article on page 27, some people want a new highway to be built but others do not. It's important to understand what everyone thinks—and why—in order to make the best decision.

Read the article and answer the following questions.

Who thinks a new highway should be built?

a) Alice Schwartz, president of the Monaro Residents' Committee

b) the elders of the Ngarigo people

c) Bill Thomas, environmental activist

d) the writer of the article

Why do they think a new highway is needed?

a) to boost tourism to the area

b) to provide an escape route during a bushfire

c) to provide jobs for road builders

d) to enrich the environment

The Ngarigo people think that ...

a) a new highway is necessary.

b) there are already enough roads.

c) bushfires are nothing to worry about.

d) the proposed highway would harm sacred land.

Social awareness

4 What does Bill Thomas think about the highway?

a) It will save lives.

b) It should be moved to a different location.

c) It should not be built at all.

d) It should only be two lanes wide.

5 People's views are shaped by their experiences.

True False

6 People should not be allowed to say what they think.

True False

7 It is important to try to understand other people's views.

True False

Your view

8 Do you think a new highway should be built? Why or why not?

English – Literature

Australian Curriculum Links: *ACELT1596, ACELT1603*

Highway – no way!

Isn't it a crime

Gouging out the ground

Harming animals, trees, plants

Without a second glance

As if all that matters is

You

Read the poem above and answer the following questions.

1 What type of poem is this?

a) rhyming
b) free form
c) acrostic
d) haiku

2 Who may have written the poem?

a) a member of the Monaro Residents' Association
b) an elder of the Ngarigo people
c) a government official
d) an environmental activist

Social awareness

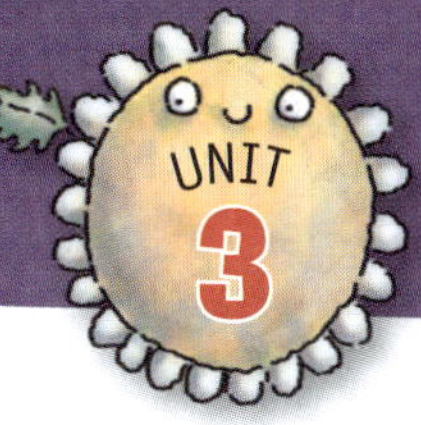

The poet has strong views about the new highway.

True False

Writing poetry is a good way to express yourself and show how you feel.

True False

The poet is in favour of the proposal.

True False

What is the purpose of the poem?

____

____

7. The poet uses expressive language to communicate their viewpoint. List three words from the poem that show how they feel about the proposed highway.

______________ ______________ ______________

Your view

8. Do you agree or disagree with the poet? Why?

____

____

____

____

____

____

____

____

____

____

HASS – Geography

Australian Curriculum Links: *ACHASSI059, ACHASSI081, ACHASSK069, ACHASSK089, ACHASSK090*

For tens of thousands of years, Australian Aboriginal peoples have adapted to the natural resources of their Country/Place. Their deep spiritual connection to their home means that they care for the land on which they live. Aboriginal land management practices are sustainable—people take what they need while protecting the environment for the benefit of future generations.

Traditional burning techniques have allowed Australian Aboriginal people to successfully manage their land. Known as 'fire-stick farming', controlled fires burn dry leaves, undergrowth and bushes. This provides the soil with nutrients and makes room for new plants to grow.

After the 2020 bushfires, many people suggested we incorporate traditional practices into our fire-prevention efforts. This would lead to more regular burning, reducing the amount of material that could otherwise result in hard-to-control bushfires.

Answer the following questions.

Traditional Aboriginal land management practices are sustainable.

True False

It's necessary to sacrifice the future for the sake of people who are alive today.

True False

Fire-stick farming is a fire hazard and should be stopped.

True False

Non-indigenous Australians can learn a lot about fire management from Australian Aboriginal people.

True False

How would removing dried leaves and bushes help stop bushfires getting out of control?

____

____

TARGETING GENERAL CAPABILITIES YEARS 3-4 © PASCAL PRESS ISBN: 9781925726220

6 How does the burning of leaves and undergrowth benefit the soil?

7 What does it mean to 'incorporate traditional practices into our fire-prevention strategies'?

Your view

8 Imagine that you live in the Snowy Monaro region. You have discovered that the Ngarigo people have long known how to manage fires. You meet Alice Schwartz, president of the Monaro Residents' Association. What would you say to her?

HASS – Civics and Citizenship

Australian Curriculum Links: *ACHASSK072, ACHASSK091*

Australia has three levels of government: federal, state and local. Local governments are closest to the people. They provide basic services that are used every day, including swimming pools, libraries, garbage collection and local roads.

Local governments have a duty to protect the environment. This involves taking steps to stop businesses and individuals from polluting, as well as promoting recycling. Local governments also need to make sure interested members of the community have the opportunity to take part in conservation efforts.

Not everybody agrees with how things should be done, however. When making decisions, local governments consider opposing views. They host community meetings where people can discuss various issues. Community participation allows residents to contribute to society and have a say in the matters that they care about.

Answer the following questions.

Which level of government is responsible for basic, everyday services such as garbage collection, libraries and swimming pools?

a) federal government

b) local government

c) state government

d) regional government

Local governments ...

a) aim to keep pollution levels low.

b) are the main polluters in society.

c) encourage conservation efforts.

d) a and c.

TARGETING GENERAL CAPABILITIES YEARS 3-4 © PASCAL PRESS ISBN: 9781925726220

3 **Local governments encourage businesses and individuals to harm the environment.**

True False

4 **Local governments provide recycling facilities.**

True False

5 **Local governments are responsible for local roads.**

True False

6 **Local governments do not take community views into account when making decisions.**

True False

7 **List three people or groups of people that you believe should attend the Snowy Monaro community meeting about bushfire strategies.**

______________ ______________ ______________

Your view

8 **Four-lane highways are the responsibility of state governments, not local. Do you think it would still be worth having a Snowy Monaro community meeting to discuss the proposed new highway? Why or why not?**

Health & Physical Education

Australian Curriculum Links: *ACPPS037, ACPPS038*

Healthy relationships are formed when people respect other's opinions. They don't have to always agree, but it helps if they try to understand each other. Allowing people to express themselves is the first step. If they're not allowed to speak out, they may feel that their views are not valued.

Societies often face challenges or hardships, such as bushfires. These hardships can bring people together, but they can also tear them apart. Working together to solve a common problem can unite people who hold different views. It's important to look for common ground. Even if people can't agree on every single detail, it may be possible to find a compromise solution that everybody can accept.

Read the news article on page 27 and answer the following questions.

Alice Schwartz respects the views of the Ngarigo people as she is prepared to work with them to find a new place for the highway.

True False

The Ngarigo people feel that their concerns are being listened to.

True False

Bill Thomas wants to find a solution that everybody is happy with.

True False

Everyone actually wants the same thing – a good, safe environment to live in.

True False

Finding a solution that everybody is happy with is too much effort.

True False

TARGETING GENERAL CAPABILITIES YEARS 3-4 © PASCAL PRESS ISBN: 9781925726220

Your views

6 Do you think that stopping people from expressing their opinion is a form of bullying? Why or why not?

7 What do you think is the best solution to the new highway issue?

8 Discuss your ideas in a group. Did the others agree with you? Were your views respected? How did that make you feel?

Self-reflection

This unit was about social awareness. What have you learnt about people respecting each other's opinions?

A MESSAGE FROM THE PRIME MINISTER

Good evening Australia. Tonight, I want to talk to you about COVID-19 and what it means for you. The coronavirus that causes this disease has spread to many countries around the world, with some hit harder than others. We are lucky to have reacted quickly to the situation, and so far, our nation has dealt with the threat well.

Most Australians who catch the disease will only experience a mild or moderate illness. However, elderly people and those with existing health problems are much more vulnerable and at risk of suffering a severe illness or even death. COVID-19 is a contagious disease, and because this is a new coronavirus, nobody is immune. That is why we are taking steps to protect the lives of vulnerable members within our community.

We've closed our borders. We've brought Australians back from virus hotspots and placed them safely in quarantine, but it's important to realise we all have a part to play. There are now further limits to most indoor and outdoor gatherings. We ask that you stay at home unless you are:

- going to work or school
- shopping for essential supplies, such as food or medicine
- exercising in your neighbourhood
- attending medical appointments or providing care.

Please respect social distancing measures and stay at least 1.5 metres away from other people. Avoid physical greetings such as shaking hands, hugging and kissing, and steer away from crowds. Be sure to practise good hygiene, and self-isolate if you have been in contact with someone who's recently returned from overseas or who has COVID-19.

If we all follow the rules, together we can beat this disease and protect Australia. Thank you.

TARGETING GENERAL CAPABILITIES YEARS 3-4 © PASCAL PRESS ISBN: 9781925726220

English – Language

Australian Curriculum Links: *ACELA1476, ACELA1477, ACELA1488, ACELA1489*

To communicate well, it's important to use the right words. People use language differently depending on who it is they are talking to. You speak one way when you talk to your teacher and another way when you speak with your friends. It will be different again when you talk to your parents or grandparents. Depending on who you're talking to, you might speak formally, using proper words and grammar, or casually, using slang words and informal sentences.

The words you choose will also depend on how you want people to respond. You might want to be persuasive, entertaining or informative—or all three! Some words and sentences simply state facts, while others are emotional and aim to make listeners feel or behave in a certain way.

Read the Prime Minister's speech on page 38 and answer the following questions.

Why did the Prime Minister make this speech?

a) to provide information

b) to persuade listeners to follow instructions

c) to entertain the public

d) a and b

Why does the Prime Minister start his speech with 'Good evening Australia'?

a) He wants to tell listeners the time.

b) To show he is talking to everyone, not just one particular group.

c) To show that he is feeling good.

d) He could not come up with a better beginning.

Social management

The Prime Minister wants Australians to ...

a) take the COVID-19 threat seriously and follow instructions.

b) not worry about COVID-19 and live life as usual.

c) pay more money to support our hospitals.

d) migrate to New Zealand.

The Prime Minister's speech is ...

a) very formal, as if he is talking to the Queen.

b) very informal, as if he is having a private chat with his best friend.

c) formal, but still conversational and friendly.

d) informal, as well as bossy and threatening.

Word bank

lucky new safely illness risk
beat threat vulnerable contagious

Answer the following questions using words from the speech's word bank.

Which words describe the plain facts of the coronavirus?

______________ ______________ ______________

Which emotional words try to convince people to follow the rules?

______________ ______________ ______________

Which words are used to help reassure the public?

______________ ______________ ______________

Your view

Do you think the Prime Minister made an effective speech? Why or why not?

____

____

____

TARGETING GENERAL CAPABILITIES YEARS 3-4 © PASCAL PRESS ISBN: 9781925726220

HASS - Civics and Citizenship

Australian Curriculum Links: *ACHASSI080, ACHASSK092*

Sometimes the difference between rules and laws can be confusing. 'Laws' can only be passed by governments and they apply to everyone in society. For example, it's against the law to steal. If a law is broken, the legal system may impose a punishment. This could be a fine or time in jail. The social distancing measures imposed during the COVID-19 outbreak were laws. People who broke them were sometimes fined, especially if they refused to cooperate with police when warned.

'Rules' are set by many different bodies. Schools can set rules—so can sports clubs, religious groups and even families. Your school has rules about uniforms, and sports clubs have rules about how the game is played. Your family might have rules about how long you can spend on devices. Rules apply only to people who belong to these groups. If you break a rule, you won't be punished by the government or go to jail! However, you might get school detention, be kicked off the team or have your mobile phone confiscated by your parents.

Rules and laws exist to make sure that everybody's rights are recognised. They help resolve conflicts and protect the vulnerable.

Answer the following questions.

Laws can only be passed by governments.

True False

Laws do not apply to everyone in society.

True False

The punishment for breaking a rule is the same as for breaking a law.

True False

Rules can be set by ...

a) the government only.

b) your school.

c) a sports club.

d) b and c.

Social management

Rules versus laws

Wear a school hat outdoors. Don't speed while driving.
Don't go through red lights. No bombing in the pool.
No trespassing. Eat dinner before dessert.

5 **Which of the above are rules?**

____

____

6 **Which of the above are laws?**

____

____

7 **The social distancing laws during the COVID-19 outbreak were introduced to ...**

a) punish people who did not follow them.

b) reduce the number of people who got sick.

c) protect vulnerable members of society.

d) b and c.

Your view

8 **People who broke the social distancing laws were not always fined, especially if they obeyed the police when warned. Do you think they should have been fined anyway? Why or why not?**

____

____

____

____

TARGETING GENERAL CAPABILITIES YEARS 3-4 © PASCAL PRESS ISBN: 9781925726220

Mathematics – Statistics and Probability

Australian Curriculum Links: *ACMSP069, ACMSP070, ACMSP095, ACMSP096*

During the COVID-19 outbreak, the government gave advice on how to practise good hand hygiene. This is because the coronavirus spread when someone touched a contaminated surface and then touched their face. Most people followed good hand hygiene during the outbreak, but how careful are they the rest of the time? One way to find out is to collect and analyse data.

Fill in your answers for this Hand Hygiene Survey by ticking the correct boxes below (one for each question). Then collect all the answers of your classmates, but to keep things private, tell them not to write their names on the questionnaires.

(a) When you cough, where do you do it?

☐ open air ☐ hands ☐ elbow ☐ tissue

(b) Do you wash your hands before eating?

☐ never ☐ sometimes ☐ often ☐ always

(c) Do you wash your hands after going to the toilet?

☐ never ☐ sometimes ☐ often ☐ always

(d) How important do you think hand hygiene is?

☐ very ☐ mostly ☐ a bit ☐ not important

Social management

Once you have the data, you need to keep track of it. An easy way is to see how many people selected each category. For example, Rachel surveyed her class and organised the data for survey question (a) using tally marks like this:

Place where people cough (i.e. the categories)	Number of students (i.e. the tally marks)
open air	||||
hands	𝍸 |
elbows	𝍸 𝍸 ||
tissue	𝍸 |||

Use the tally tables below to organise the data for your class.

Survey question (a)

Place where people cough	Number of students
open air	
hands	
elbows	
tissue	

Survey question (b)

Washing hands before eating	Number of students
never	
sometimes	
often	
always	

TARGETING GENERAL CAPABILITIES YEARS 3-4 © PASCAL PRESS ISBN: 9781925726220

Survey question (c)

Washing hands after toilet	Number of students
never	
sometimes	
often	
always	

Survey question (d)

Attitudes to hand hygiene	Number of students
very important	
mostly important	
a bit important	
not important	

It's much easier to make sense of your data if you display it in a graph. For instance, look at the bar graph that Rachel created using the results of her class's survey question (a):

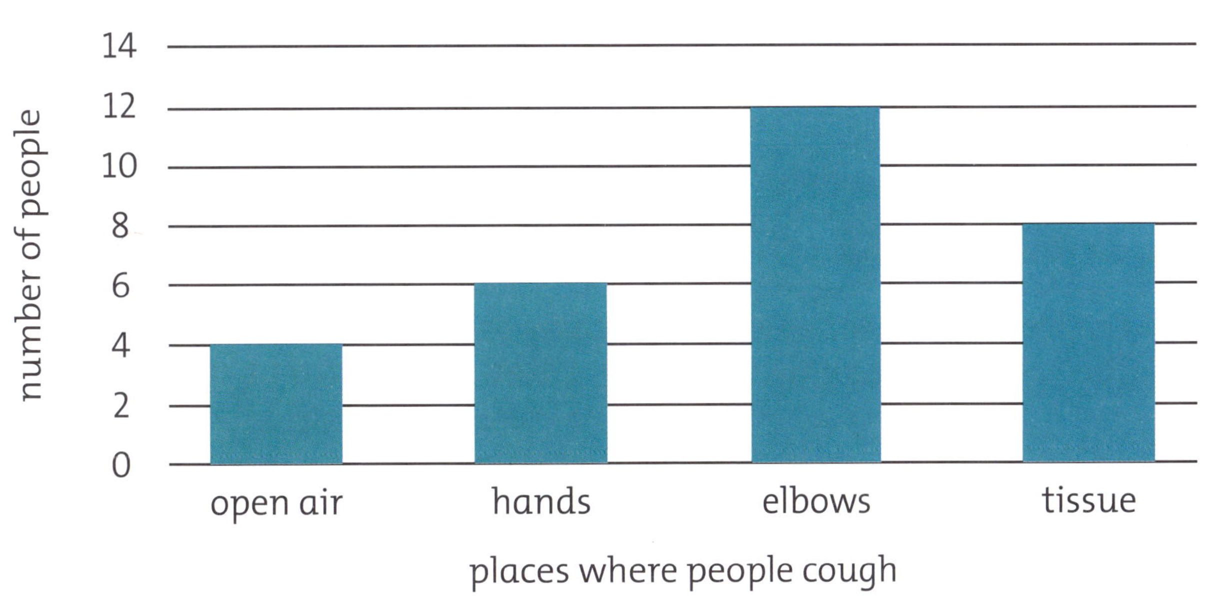

Social management

Answer the following questions using Rachel's graph.

What type of graph is this?

a) pie chart
c) bar graph
b) roll chart
d) line graph

What information is given by the vertical axis?

a) the number of times a category was picked

b) the category

What information is given by the horizontal axis?

a) the number of times a category was picked

b) the category

How many students in Rachel's class cough into their hands?

a) 4 b) 6 c) 12 d) 8

Which is the most common place for her classmates to cough?

___

Which is the least common place for her classmates to cough?

___

How many more students cough into their elbows than into their hands? Show your working out.

___

Your class

Create a graph for your class survey results. Be sure to fill in all the information: graph and axis titles, numbers and categories.

TARGETING GENERAL CAPABILITIES YEARS 3-4 © PASCAL PRESS ISBN: 9781925726220

Technologies – Digital Technologies

Australian Curriculum Links: *ACTDIP012, ACTDIP013*

Rachel was so proud of her survey results, she decided to publish her data online. She shared everything on social media: the survey questions, the tally tables and the graphs. In fact, she was so excited she named all the people who took part in the survey and even identified who had said what. She was able to do this because they had written their names on the questionnaires. Rachel did not think she had done anything wrong—she was just sharing a fun class activity.

However, her classmate Leo was not so pleased. He didn't like the fact that he was identified as being someone who did not cover their coughs, wash their hands or care about hygiene. He felt that he was being publicly shamed.

Things got worse when Mary, a girl in their class, confronted him and accused him of spreading germs. Leo was so upset he wanted to change schools.

Answer the following questions.

Online material can change the way that people think.

True False

Online material can change the way that people behave.

True False

Online material can have both good and bad effects on people.

True False

Rachel should have considered how her classmates might feel before naming them.

True False

There is no point in trying to protect people's privacy online.

True False

How should the survey have been conducted to protect the students' identities?

____

____

Social management

7 What should Rachel have done before publishing the survey results online?

Your view

8 Leo has now started practising good hand hygiene. Do you think Rachel's actions were justified after all? What might have been a better way to encourage Leo to do the right thing?

Self-reflection

This unit was about social management. What have you learnt about working with others to reach important goals?

PERSONAL & SOCIAL CAPABILITY

TARGETING GENERAL CAPABILITIES YEARS 3-4 © PASCAL PRESS ISBN: 9781925726220

Self-awareness assessment

Recognise emotions

How does the thought of walking to school each day make you feel? Circle the words below that apply to you. You can pick more than one!

excited   happy   nervous   tired   scared   sad

angry   joyful   anxious   irritated   impatient   content

2 Why did you choose these words?

___

___

3 The cartoon on page 8 contains information about why young children may have trouble crossing roads safely. Do you agree or disagree with the cartoon's message? Explain.

___

___

___

___

Recognise personal qualities and achievements and develop reflective practice

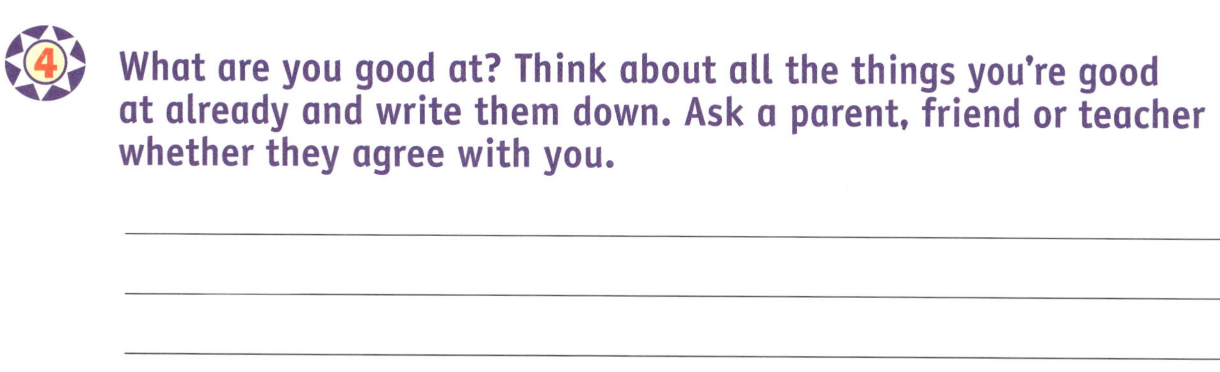

4 What are you good at? Think about all the things you're good at already and write them down. Ask a parent, friend or teacher whether they agree with you.

___

___

___

___

5 There's always room to improve—for everyone. What new things would you like to be able to do, and which skills do you want to develop?

____

____

____

____

Understand self as learner

6 **There are different ways to learn and different types of learners. These include:**

- seeing learners – who like to see images
- hearing learners – who like to hear explanations
- writing learners – who like to read texts
- doing learners – who learn best by doing things.

The list below shows different ways of learning. Put them in the right places in the table.

Read book   Listen to teacher   Look at diagrams

Listen to podcast   Look at infographics   Follow demonstration

Write notes   Perform experiment

Seeing learners	Hearing learners	Writing learners	Doing learners

7 **Which type of learner are you? Why do you think that?**

____

____

____

____

TARGETING GENERAL CAPABILITIES YEARS 3-4 © PASCAL PRESS ISBN: 9781925726220

Self-management assessment

Express emotions appropriately

Image by photosavvy is licensed under CC BY-ND 2.0

1. The girl in the photograph has just finished a swimming race. It was very important to her, and she had been training for many months. Do you think she won? Why or why not?

2. Describe a time in your life when you may have felt the same way.

Develop self-discipline and set goals

3 If the girl in the photograph was your best friend, what advice would you have for her? How would you encourage her to achieve her goals?

____

____

____

____

Work independently and show initiative

4 Look at the words and phrases below. Circle the ones that you think can help people achieve their goals.

give up   get upset   keep trying   blame someone

be positive   ask for help   say it's too hard   take a chance

learn more   throw a tantrum   enjoy the process   cry

Become confident, resilient and adaptable

5 Write down an important goal that you have right now.

____

____

____

____

6 What can you do if your first attempt to achieve that goal does not succeed?

____

____

____

____

TARGETING GENERAL CAPABILITIES YEARS 3-4 © PASCAL PRESS ISBN: 9781925726220

Social awareness assessment

Appreciate diverse perspectives

1. There are three different viewpoints expressed in the article on page 27. What does each group want and why do they want this? Fill in the table.

Who?	What do they want?	Why?
Monaro Residents' Association		
The Ngarigo people		
Environmental activists		

2. Which group do you agree with?

3. Argue the case from the point of view of somebody that you DO NOT agree with.

Contribute to civil society

4. Everyone can contribute to civil society by expressing their views and having their voice heard. In the space below, draft an email to the local council, supporting the view that you most agree with.

Understand relationships

Many factors contribute to positive relationships in community meetings. Use words from the word bank to find things that make a positive contribution and things that are negative. Fill in the table.

Word bank

discussing ignoring sarcasm listening
interrupting patience shouting taking turns
applauding booing

Positive effect	Negative effect

TARGETING GENERAL CAPABILITIES YEARS 3-4 © PASCAL PRESS ISBN: 9781925726220

Social management assessment

Communicate effectively and work collaboratively

1. Read the Prime Minister's speech on page 38. The Prime Minister wanted everyone to work together to fight COVID-19. Write your own short speech aimed at your classmates, encouraging them to help stop the spread of a disease.

Make decisions

2. What sorts of things do you think the government considered when restricting people's freedom to go out?

Negotiate and resolve conflict

The government's decision caused a lot of conflict in society. Some people thought the laws were harsh and unnecessary, others thought they didn't go far enough. It isn't always possible to avoid conflict, but there are things we can do to help find solutions.

Unjumble the words in the sentences below to discover what they are. The first letter of each word is given to you.

i. It is important to **pexilan** the reasons for a decision. e________

ii. People should have the chance to **ltka** about how they feel. t________

iii. It is important to **tselin** to different points of view. l________

iv. Even if we disagree, we should still **repetsc** other's views. r________

v. The aim is to find a solution that **toms** people are happy with. m________

Develop leadership skills

The government had to take a strong leadership role to help the nation deal with COVID-19. Can you think of other situations when laws as strict as these may be appropriate?

Hint: Think about some other sorts of crises that nations might face.

____

____

____

____

TARGETING GENERAL CAPABILITIES YEARS 3-4 © PASCAL PRESS ISBN: 9781925726220

Intercultural Understanding

Intercultural understanding encourages children to be aware of the importance of becoming responsible global citizens by enhancing cultural knowledge. As outlined in the curriculum, the elements and sub-elements are:

Recognising culture and developing respect: investigate culture and cultural identity; explore and compare cultural knowledge, beliefs and practices; develop respect for cultural diversity

Interacting and empathising with others: communicate across cultures; consider and develop multiple perspectives; empathise with others

Reflecting on intercultural experiences and taking responsibility: reflect on intercultural experiences; challenge stereotypes and prejudices; mediate cultural difference.

VASILOPITA

Every New Year's Day, Greek families around the world enjoy the centuries-old tradition of sharing a vasilopita. It may sound similar to other traditions you've encountered, but it has unique origins.

Vasilopita means 'Basil pie', and it's named after a saint. Back in the fourth century AD, Basil was a bishop. He called on the citizens of Caesarea (now in modern-day Turkey) to raise money to stop a siege. They gave everything they had, and according to the story, the enemy felt ashamed and withdrew. Basil was given the task of returning the gold and jewels to their owners.

However, he had no way of knowing who had given what. Legend has it that everything was baked into loaves of bread, which were distributed among the citizens. Variations of the story exist, but the most common one is that each family got back their original possessions!

Vasilopita is still baked and enjoyed by families every year. Different parts of Greece have different varieties. Some versions are cake-like, while others resemble a sweet bread similar to a brioche. The number of the new year is often written on the top with an edible ingredient, such as slivered almonds or icing sugar. Whatever the recipe, all vasilopitas share a common feature: a coin is always baked into the loaf to commemorate Saint Basil.

On New Year's Day, the vasilopita is cut into slices. It's distributed among family and guests according to age, the eldest getting the first piece. Whoever finds the coin is said to have good luck for the rest of the year!

TARGETING GENERAL CAPABILITIES YEARS 3-4 © PASCAL PRESS ISBN: 9781925726220

English – Language

Australian Curriculum Links: *ACELA1478, ACELA1479, ACELA1480, ACELA1487, ACELA1490*

The text on page 58 investigates the origins and performance of a New Year tradition that is enjoyed in Greece and in other countries throughout the world, including Australia.

Read the text and answer the following questions.

What type of text is it?

a) imaginative

b) informative

c) persuasive

d) all of the above

What is the purpose of the text?

a) to encourage people to eat vasilopitas

b) to share an understanding of culture

c) to warn against the hazard of choking on coins

d) to show people how to avoid a siege

The text is divided up into ...

a) paragraphs.

b) bullet points.

c) steps.

d) ingredients.

4 **What is meant by a topic sentence? Find an example in the text and write it down.**

5 **Circle the correct words in the following sentences.**

In the text, the writer uses the words you've and it's. They are examples of **contractions / possessives.** *Their use suggests that the text is* **formal / informal.**

6 **Which language does the word 'vasilopita' come from and what does it mean?**

7 **Which word, now common in Australia, recently came from another language?**

a) bread

b) cake

c) brioche

d) none of the above

Your view

8 **The writer of the text says, 'It may sound similar to other traditions you've encountered'. Are you familiar with any other cultural tradition that involves baking a coin in a cake? What is it?**

TARGETING GENERAL CAPABILITIES YEARS 3-4 © PASCAL PRESS ISBN: 9781925726220

HASS – History

Australian Curriculum Links: *ACHASSK063, ACHASSK065, ACHASSI077*

Chinese New Year falls on a different day each year, somewhere between late January and early February. Its date isn't determined by the modern calendar, but rather by the cycles of the moon, which is why it's also called the Lunar New Year. Another name for it is the Spring Festival because it marks the approach of spring in China. Chinese New Year celebrations last for days and include:

- putting up red decorations in streets and homes
- spending time with family
- the lighting of firecrackers
- the giving of gifts, where children receive red envelopes containing money.

Chinese New Year festivals can be traced back over 3000 years. They originated with the myth of Nian, a monster that attacked people and property on New Year's Eve. To scare him off, people would make loud noises with crackling bamboo (later replaced with firecrackers) and place red scrolls on doors and windows to stop the monster from entering.

Over time, the celebrations have evolved. They've spread to other countries, including Australia, and everyone is able to enjoy the street parades and sample the food.

Read the text and answer the following questions.

Chinese New Year falls on 1 January each year.

True False

Chinese New Year traditions date back at least 3000 years.

True False

Chinese New Year is also known as the Luna New Year because …

a) the date varies each year.

b) it is connected with the cycles of the moon.

c) it marks the start of spring in China.

d) it marks the start of spring in Australia.

Which tradition is NOT associated with Chinese New Year?

a) putting up red decorations

b) sharing vasilopita with family

c) lighting firecrackers

d) giving money-filled red envelopes to children

According to the legend, what was the mythical monster Nian frightened of?

a) loud noises

b) red objects

c) large families

d) a and b

Why do you think Chinese New Year is celebrated in Australia?

____

____

Greek and Chinese New Year's celebrations are very different, but they have some important similarities. What are they?

____

____

Your view

The Chinese zodiac is based on a 12-year cycle, and each year is represented by an animal. For instance, 2020 marked the Year of the Rat, and 2021 is the Year of the Ox. Zodiac animals are used to tell people's fortune, and they depend on the year you were born. Do you know your zodiac animal?

____

TARGETING GENERAL CAPABILITIES YEARS 3-4 © PASCAL PRESS ISBN: 9781925726220

HASS – Geography

Australian Curriculum Links: *ACHASSK067, ACHASSI073, ACHASSI078, ACHASSK088*

The Pacific Islands are what we call the islands found in the Pacific Ocean. Some of these are very close to Australia, such as New Zealand, Indonesia and Papua New Guinea. Although they are close, they are very different to Australia in many ways.

Country	Australia	New Zealand	Papua New Guinea	Indonesia
Capital city	Canberra	Wellington	Port Moresby	Jakarta
Population	24 million	4.6 million	7.9 million	264 million
Land size	7.69 million km^2	268 000 km^2	462 800 km^2	1.90 million km^2
Main languages	English	English, Maori	English, Hiri Motu, Tok Pisin	Indonesian
Currency	Australian dollar	New Zealand dollar	Papua New Guinea kina	Indonesian rupiah
Highest mountain	Mount Kosciusko	Mount Cook	Mount Wilhelm	Puncak Jaya

Source: Australian Geography Centres: *Middle Primary*, p.11, Blake Education

Recognising culture & developing respect

INTERCULTURAL UNDERSTANDING

Look at the map and table and answer the following questions.

Which country has the smallest population?

___

Which country does NOT include English as one of its main languages?

___

Which country has three main languages?

___

Indonesia has more than ten times Australia's population, but it is much smaller in land size. There are 10 million people living in the capital, Jakarta, alone. If you visited Jakarta, would you expect it to be more crowded or less crowded than an Australian city? Why?

___

The Aboriginal and Torres Strait Islander peoples are indigenous to Australia. Which peoples are indigenous to New Zealand?

Hint: Look at the table entry for languages spoken.

___

Although Australia is in the Pacific, much of our population originally came from countries much further away.

True False

Australia enjoys the cultures and traditions of people from all around the world, including our Pacific neighbours.

True False

Your view

Which Pacific Island would you most like to visit? Why would you like to go there?

___

___

___

TARGETING GENERAL CAPABILITIES YEARS 3-4 © PASCAL PRESS ISBN: 9781925726220

Technologies – Design and Technology

Australian Curriculum Link: *ACTDEK012*

One of the main ingredients in Greek new year bread (vasilopita) is wheat flour. Wheat is a type of grass with edible seeds. It started off as a wild grass, but through selective planting over thousands of years it evolved into the ancestor of our modern grain. Originating in the Middle East, its use has spread throughout the world.

Traditionally, much of the work was done by hand. The wheat was harvested with a sickle. The seeds were threshed (separated from the inedible chaff) by beating them, then ground into flour between large stones. These methods are still used in traditional societies, but the process is highly mechanised in modern societies such as Australia. Giant combines harvest and thresh the wheat, which goes to a mill to be made into flour. White flour is more processed than wholemeal because more of the wheat's bran (its outer layer) is removed.

Wheat is one of Australia's main crops, and the map shows where it's grown. It is harvested in spring and summer, and most of it is sent to Asia and the Middle East.

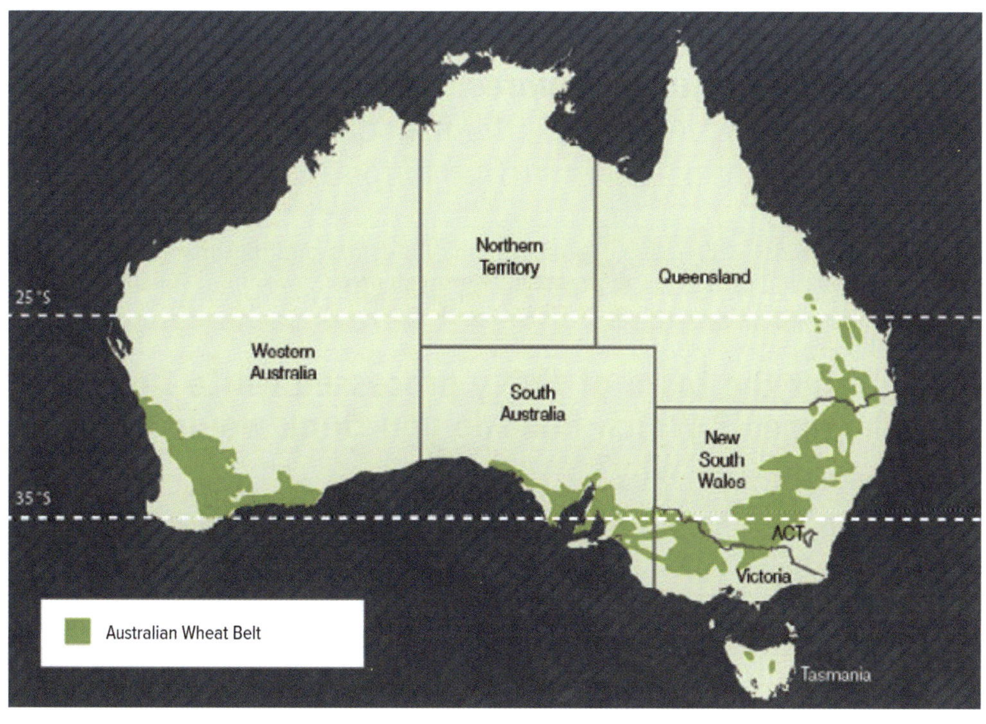

Recognising culture & developing respect

Read the text and answer the following questions.

Wheat grows on a type of ...

a) tree.
b) vine.
c) root.
d) grass.

Where did wheat originate?

a) Australia
b) Asia
c) the Middle East
d) a Pacific Island

A sickle is a type of ...

a) hand tool.
b) machine.
c) ancient grain.
d) stone used to grind flour.

Threshing involves separating the edible seed from the inedible chaff.

True False

Australia uses mainly traditional methods to produce flour.

True False

Look at the map. In which states is wheat grown?

Which type of country would produce more wheat, a modern society like Australia or a more traditional one? Explain.

Your view

Do you prefer the taste of finely processed white flour or the more rustic wholemeal? Which flour do you think would work best when making vasilopita? Why?

Hint: Remember vasilopita is similar to a sweet bread or a cake.

TARGETING GENERAL CAPABILITIES YEARS 3-4 © PASCAL PRESS ISBN: 9781925726220

Health & Physical Education

Australian Curriculum Link: *ACTPPS037, ACPPS042*

All cultures enjoy special foods at important times of the year as a way to celebrate their identity. The foods may differ, but they all serve the same basic purpose: to pass on a culture's beliefs, traditions and values.

Gulab jamun

Christmas pudding

Baklava

Mooncake

Vasilopita

Draw lines to match the celebration food with its place of origin.

Gulab jamun	China
Vasilopita	United Kingdom
Baklava	Greece
Mooncake	Middle East
Christmas Pudding	India

Word bank

Christmas Eid Diwali New Year Mid-Autumn Festival

Using the above information and your knowledge of different cultures, identify the relevant festivals listed in the word bank.

2 **Christmas pudding** ______________________

3 **Vasilopita** ______________________

4 **Baklava** ______________________

5 **Mooncake** ______________________

6 **Gulab jamun** ______________________

7 **Which of these foods, if any, have you eaten? Did you like them?**

____

____

Your view

8 **Think about your own cultural heritage. Do you and your family have any special foods that you eat to mark celebrations or important events? What are they?**

____

____

____

Self-reflection

This unit was about recognising culture and developing respect. What have you learnt about respecting the traditions of other cultures?

____

____

____

TARGETING GENERAL CAPABILITIES YEARS 3-4 © PASCAL PRESS ISBN: 9781925726220

Australian Aboriginal peoples tell stories to explain the world around us. These are called 'creation stories', and these acts of creation are often referred to as 'The Dreaming'. Aboriginal culture is an oral culture, which means that none of these stories were written down until recently. Instead, they were passed down through families and Elders by being told. Dreaming stories are passed down not only through storytelling, but through song, dance and artwork.

Many Dreaming stories explain the creation of the Australian landscape. The Rainbow Serpent is an ancestral creation being that appears in many Aboriginal Dreaming stories. These stories describe how the Rainbow Serpent created various features of the Australian landscape, such as gorges, mountains, rivers and billabongs.

Different Aboriginal language groups have different names for the Rainbow Serpent.

Name for the Rainbow Serpent	Language group	Location
Almudj	Gagudju	Northern Territory
Warrajum	Mununjali	Queensland
Bolung	Jawoyn	Northern Territory
Wawi	Wiradjuri	Central New South Wales
Waugyl	Noongar	Western Australia

These are just four locations around Australia with Aboriginal Dreaming stories about the Rainbow Serpent related to their creation.

The Gagudju people of the Northern Territory believe that the Rainbow Serpent still rests in Kakadu National Park and should not be disturbed.

Source: Australian Geography Centres: Middle Primary, p.9, Blake Education

Barron Gorge, Queensland

Wolfe Creek Crater, Western Australia

Kakadu National Park, Northern Territory

Ancient Aboriginal art of the Rainbow Serpent at Mt Coot-tha, Queensland

English – Language

Australian Curriculum Links: *ACELA1475, ACELA1487*

Many different cultures throughout history have used creation stories to explain how the world was made. Although they vary, they share many similarities. They all try to explain how the world came to be and why it is the way it is. Often there is a moral to be learnt and a sense of wisdom to be gained. Many words from these stories have even become part of our modern language, such as 'chaos', a goddess from an ancient Greek creation story.

Most creation stories started off as oral traditions, passed down through the generations over hundreds and even thousands of years. They've been passed on by storytelling, poetry, song, dance and art. The stories are so powerful that they are still told today. They represent who people are and where they came from. By sharing stories, people of different cultures get to know and understand each other better.

Read the information on page 69 and answer the following questions.

1 What are creation stories?

____

____

2 What is 'The Dreaming'?

____

____

3 Many different cultures throughout history have creation stories.

True False

4 Creation stories were carefully written down at the time when they were first told.

True False

TARGETING GENERAL CAPABILITIES YEARS 3-4 © PASCAL PRESS ISBN: 9781925726220

5 What do the Rainbow Serpent stories describe?

a) how the kangaroo got its tail

b) how the kookaburra got its laugh

c) how mountains, rivers and billabongs were created

d) how the emu got its feathers

6 Why do you think there are different Aboriginal names for the Rainbow Serpent?

Hint: Look closely at the table on page 69.

____

____

____

7 In the past, as well as today, stories can be told in many different ways. These can be oral (spoken), visual (seen) or written. The word bank shows different ways of telling stories. Place them in the correct column of the table.

Word bank

dance poem song artwork script

novel recital movie audiobook

oral	visual	written

Your view

8 Do you know any creation stories? Describe one.

____

____

____

____

HASS – History

Australian Curriculum Links: *ACHASSK062, ACHASSK083*

When the First Peoples settled on this land at least 40 000 years ago, it was not called Australia and there were no political divisions that we call states, such as Victoria and Queensland.

It is also slightly misleading to refer to areas as 'tribal lands', although this is commonly done, because Aboriginal peoples could name a number of groups that they belonged to, not just one group. The groups were different to one another but with some common traits connecting them, such as customs and their particular language or dialect.

'Dialect' means different forms of the same language that develop over time to suit particular environments, histories and cultures. Therefore, although the various groups comprised the same 'nation', they were still separate and distinct from one another.

Aboriginal nations lived throughout the entire continent, including Tasmania, and on many of the smaller offshore islands. Each nation had its own dialogue and traditions.

Source: Blake's Australian History Guide, p.17, Blake Education

Read the text and answer the following questions.

How long have Australia's First Peoples lived in Australia?

____

Australian Aboriginal peoples divided up the land to form the states that we now recognise.

True False

Aboriginal peoples have a strong and spiritual connection to their Country/Place.

True False

Indigenous groups were different to each other but had common traits.

True False

TARGETING GENERAL CAPABILITIES YEARS 3-4 © PASCAL PRESS ISBN: 9781925726220

What is a dialect?

The traits that connected various groups of Indigenous Australians were ...

a) their customs.

b) their language or dialect.

c) their creation stories.

d) all of the above.

There is another group of Indigenous Australians that are distinct from Aboriginal peoples. Who are they?

Hint: They come from a group of islands part way between Queensland and Papua New Guinea.

Your view

8 **Have you travelled to any areas of Indigenous cultural significance? Where did you go, and what did you learn there?**

HASS – Geography

Australian Curriculum Links: *ACHASSK066, ACHASSK089*

This is the modern-day map of Australia that we all know, divided along the lines of political boundaries.

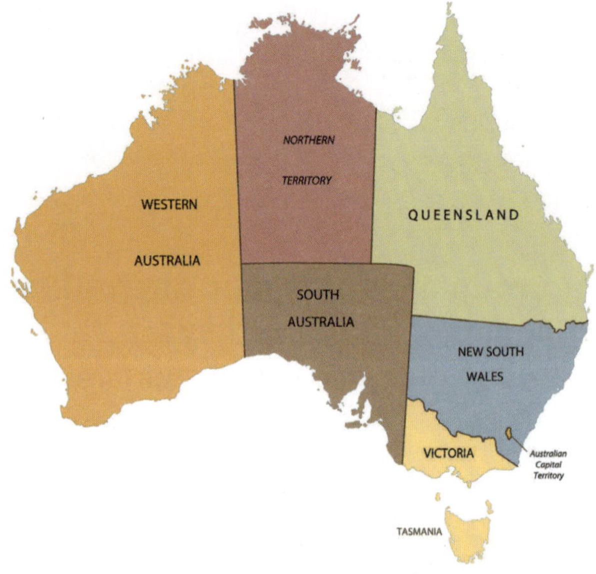

But it's only one way of looking at the country, and a very recent one at that. The map that we're familiar with was finalised as recently as the early 20th century, but Australia has been inhabited for tens of thousands of years, long before the creation of our modern nation. The Australian Institute of Aboriginal and Torres Strait Islander Studies (AIATSIS) has created a map of Indigenous Australia that attempts to represent all the language or nation groups of the Australian Indigenous peoples. As you can see, it paints a very different picture.

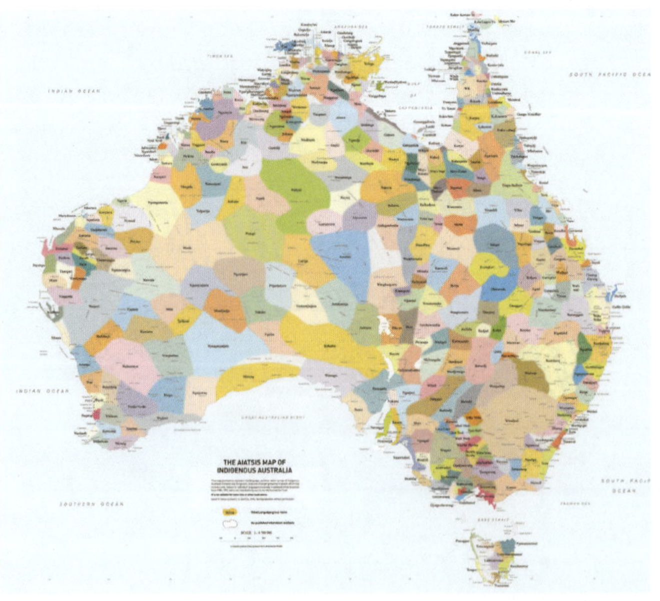

TARGETING GENERAL CAPABILITIES YEARS 3-4 © PASCAL PRESS ISBN: 9781925726220

Compare the two maps and answer the following questions.

1 Name the states and territories of modern-day Australia.

____

2 What do the boundaries on the Indigenous map represent?

____

3 The boundaries on the Indigenous map are in line with the state and territory boundaries on the modern-day political map.

True False

4 The Indigenous map shows that there are many Indigenous languages and dialects.

True False

Use words from the word bank to complete the cloze passages.

Word bank

adapted landscapes coast

5 The Indigenous map shows that Indigenous peoples lived all around Australia but were concentrated around the ____________ and rivers.

6 The Aboriginal and Torres Strait Islander Peoples ____________ their way of life to the environment of their Country/Place.

7 The photographs on page 69 show how different types of Australian ________________ are associated with Indigenous creation stories, showing their strong spiritual element.

Your view

8 Can you find the location of your hometown on the Indigenous map? Write down the name of the Indigenous custodians of the land that you live on.

____

The Arts – Visual Arts

Australian Curriculum Links: *ACAVAM110, ACAVAM113*

The Rainbow Serpent is often portrayed in Indigenous Australian art. Its shape is that of both a rainbow and a snake, showing a connection with water, rain and the seasons. There are many versions of the Rainbow Serpent story, but generally the serpent is seen as the giver of life. However, if angered, the serpent can cause devastation. Just as water is necessary for life, sometimes it can threaten it.

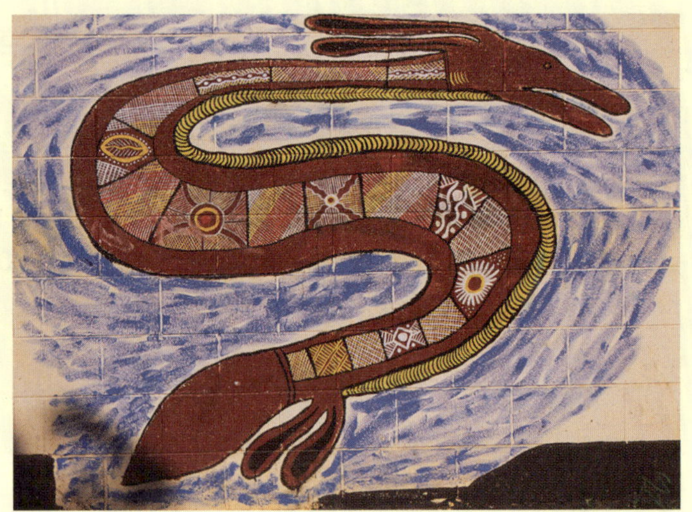

Tiwi Island mural. Photo: Bill Bachman/Alamy Stock Photo

Look at the image of the Rainbow Serpent and answer the following questions.

1 What does the shape of the image represent?

a) a rainbow

b) a billabong

c) a serpent

d) a and c

2 What was the image painted onto?

a) canvas

b) bark

c) rock

d) wood

3 What type of paint do you think the artist used?

a) natural materials such as clay

b) acrylic paints

c) oil paints

d) watercolour paints

4 Ancient Indigenous Australians used artwork as a way to tell sacred stories.

True False

5 The meaning of Indigenous artwork can be easily understood by non-Indigenous people.

True False

6 Do you enjoy looking at the image? What do you like about it?

____

____

____

7 Non-Indigenous people often look at Indigenous images as pieces of art, admiring the artists' skill and the beauty of the images. Do you think the paintings were intended that way, or did they mean something more? Explain.

____

____

____

Your turn

8 Do you have a favourite Dreaming story? Draw an image in the space below to represent your understanding of the story.

The Arts – Dance

Australian Curriculum Link: *ACADAM008*

Nambassa 1981 Arnhemland and Torres Strait dance company

Many cultures use dance as a way of telling stories. It can be easier to understand a performance if you break the dance down into four basic elements:

i. Space
Space refers to the pattern a dancer makes as they move, be it sideways, forwards, backwards or diagonally. They can be up high or down low. They can keep both feet on the floor, raise one foot, and leap. They can face the audience or turn away.

ii. Time
A dance can be fast, slow or anything in between. It can be continuous, or there can be pauses. Like music, dance has a rhythm.

iii. Dynamics
Dynamics refers to the energy level of the performance. It can be high or low, gentle or strong. Movements can be flowing or sharp, wobbly or stiff.

iv. Relationships
Dancers can dance alone or in a group. They can come together or move apart. They can reflect each other's movements, or they can perform different moves.

Look at the image and answer the following questions.

1 Dances can be used as a way of telling stories.
True False

2 Dances don't convey a deeper meaning; they are just for fun and exercise.
True False

3 Australian Aboriginals use dance as a way to communicate their beliefs and culture.

True False

4 List the four elements of dance.

____

5 Are the dancers in the picture up high or keeping low to the ground? What do you think this might indicate?

____

6 Would you expect the dancers to move flowingly, like ballerinas, or to have strong, rhythmic movements?

____

7 How would you describe the relationship of the dancers?

____

____

Your turn

8 It isn't easy to study a dance by looking at a still image—you need to see it in motion. Find a video of an Indigenous Australian dance and analyse it in terms of the four elements.

____

____

Self-reflection

This unit was about interacting and empathising with others. What have you learnt about the importance of understanding different cultures?

____

____

____

____

Reflecting on intercultural experiences & taking responsibility

INTERCULTURAL UNDERSTANDING

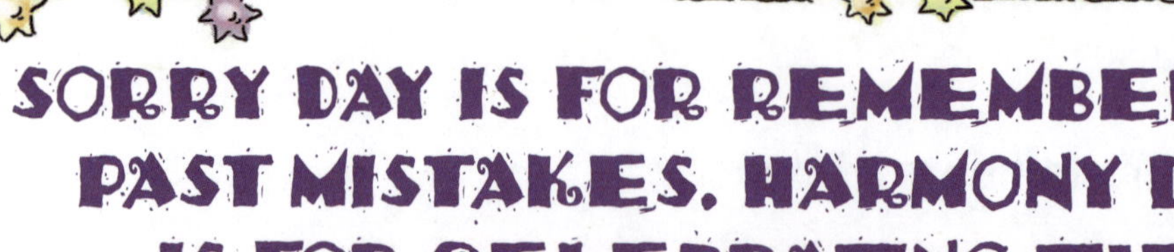

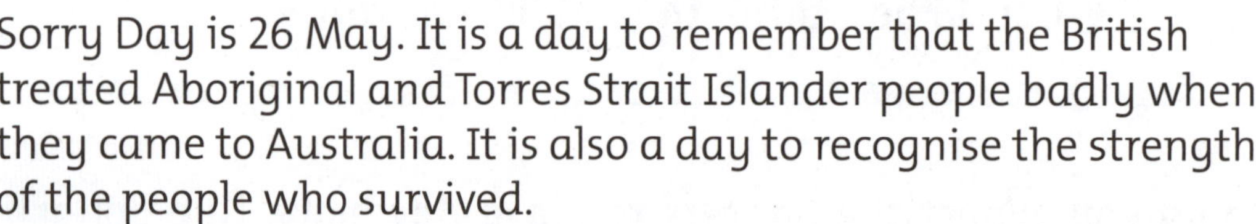

Sorry Day is 26 May. It is a day to remember that the British treated Aboriginal and Torres Strait Islander people badly when they came to Australia. It is also a day to recognise the strength of the people who survived.

The British took land belonging to Aboriginal and Torres Strait Islander peoples. They killed or hurt the people they found—sometimes on purpose and sometimes by accident. In the years that followed, the Australian government removed many Aboriginal and Torres Strait Islander children from their families. They wanted to raise them like British children. Families and communities were separated for years. Some people never returned to their families. They became known as the Stolen Generations. They told their stories in the Bringing Them Home report in 1997—the first Sorry Day was the following year. Being sorry about the past can be the first step for a better future.

Harmony Day is a chance to celebrate all the nationalities that make up Australia. It is on 21 March. It celebrates the fact that almost half of Australians were born overseas or have a parent who was. On Harmony Day, people share their culture through dance, art, film, sport, music and cooking. This allows people to learn about other cultures and teach people about their own. The message of Harmony Day is 'Everyone Belongs'.

Source: Go Facts Australia: Symbols and Celebrations, p.14, Blake Education

2019 saw the 20th anniversary of Harmony Day. It was extended to a week and renamed Harmony Week, allowing more time for the activities that celebrate diversity all across the nation.

TARGETING GENERAL CAPABILITIES YEARS 3-4 © PASCAL PRESS ISBN: 9781925726220

English – Language

Australian Curriculum Links: *ACELA1477, ACELA1478, ACELA1488, ACELA1489*

On 13 February 2008, the then Prime Minister Kevin Rudd issued a formal apology to Australia's Indigenous peoples. This is part of his historic speech:

> *The time has now come for the nation to turn a new page in Australia's history by righting the wrongs of the past and so moving forward with confidence to the future.*
>
> *We apologise for the laws and policies of successive Parliaments and governments that have inflicted profound grief, suffering and loss on these our fellow Australians.*
>
> *We apologise especially for the removal of Aboriginal and Torres Strait Islander children from their families, their communities and their country.*
>
> *For the pain, suffering and hurt of these Stolen Generations, their descendants and for their families left behind, we say sorry.*
>
> *To the mothers and the fathers, the brothers and the sisters, for the breaking up of families and communities, we say sorry.*
>
> *And for the indignity and degradation thus inflicted on a proud people and a proud culture, we say sorry.*

The former Prime Minister went on to say that parliament wants to make sure such injustices never happen again. He saw a future based on 'mutual respect, mutual resolve and mutual responsibility' in a country where all Australians, regardless of their origins, are equal partners with equal opportunities.

Source:https://parlinfo.aph.gov.au/parlInfo/search/display/display.w3p;query=Id:%22chamber/hansardr/2008-02-13/0003%22 [I think we can quote from Hansard? Or do we need permission?]

The quote is from a ...

a) movie.

b) novel.

c) poem.

d) speech.

Reflecting on intercultural experiences & taking responsibility

What is the main issue the Prime Minister apologised about?

a) Acts of parliament

b) the arrival of the British in Australia

c) the Stolen Generations

d) the lack of equal opportunity

The speech contains evaluative language—words that judge whether something is good or bad. Which of the following is NOT an example of evaluative language?

a) Australia's history

b) profound grief

c) indignity and degradation

d) proud people

The structure, flowing sentences and repetition of 'we are sorry' makes the extract sound lyrical, like a poem.

True False

The extract is informal, friendly and chatty.

True False

How is inclusive language (words and phrases that include different people) used in the extract? Give an example.

___

Is the extract using the language of opinion or the language of factual reporting?

Hint: Does it include phrases such as 'I think' and 'I believe'?

___

Your turn

Write your own speech to the Stolen Generations, sharing your thoughts about this period of Australian history.

___

___

___

INTERCULTURAL UNDERSTANDING

TARGETING GENERAL CAPABILITIES YEARS 3-4 © PASCAL PRESS ISBN: 9781925726220

HASS – History

Australian Curriculum Links: *ACHASSK064, ACHASSK086*

The Australian National Flag was created shortly after Federation, signifying the making of a new nation, but it's not the only flag we recognise. In 1971, a flag was adopted to represent Aboriginal Australians, and in 1992 a flag was adopted to recognise Torres Strait Islanders. All three are flown during special occasions: NAIDOC Week, Reconciliation Week, Mabo Day and Sorry Day. Each of these flags is rich with meaning and symbolism.

Australian National Flag

- The British Union Jack reflects the flag's origins.
- The Southern Cross shows our position in the Southern Hemisphere.
- The seven-pointed star represents the six original colonies, plus an extra point for the territories.

Aboriginal Flag

- The red stripe represents the land.
- The black stripe stands for the Aboriginal people.
- The yellow circle represents the sun.

Torres Strait Islander Flag

- The green stripes represent the land.
- The blue stripe represents the sea.
- The black stripes stand for the Torres Strait Islander people.
- In the centre is a dancer's headdress with a five-pointed star to represent the five island groups.

Reflecting on intercultural experiences & taking responsibility

INTERCULTURAL UNDERSTANDING

Look at the text and images and answer the following questions.

Which image symbolises Australia's colonial history?

a) the Southern Cross
b) the Union Jack
c) the black stripe
d) the dancer's headdress

Which image symbolises Australia's Indigenous populations?

a) the Southern Cross
b) the Union Jack
c) the black stripe
d) the dancer's headdress

Which is the most recent of the three flags?

a) the Australian National Flag
b) the Torres Strait Islander Flag
c) the Aboriginal Flag
d) They are all the same age.

British colonisation caused the death of many Indigenous Australians through conflict and disease.

True False

All of the contact between Indigenous and non-Indigenous Australians has been harmful to our First Peoples.

True False

Why do you think the Indigenous flags were created so much later than the Australian National Flag?

____

____

Why do you think all three flags are flown on special occasions such as Sorry Day?

____

____

Your turn

Use this space to design your own, all-inclusive flag. It can include elements from the Australian National Flag as well as the Aboriginal and Torres Strait Islander Flags.

TARGETING GENERAL CAPABILITIES YEARS 3-4 © PASCAL PRESS ISBN: 9781925726220

HASS – Civics and Citizenship

Australian Curriculum Links: *ACHASSK070, ACHASSK072, ACHASSK092, ACHASSK093*

Uluru, once known as Ayers Rock, has been sacred to the Anangu people for tens of thousands of years. Under their law and culture, climbing the rock was generally not permitted. However, non-Indigenous visitors began climbing Uluru as a tourist activity as far back as the 1930s.

In 1985, the Uluṟu–Kata Tjuṯa National Park was handed back to the traditional people. Although it was still legal to climb the rock, the Anangu people asked visitors to respect their culture and their wishes, and to stop climbing. Numbers slowly dropped as visitors learnt more about the Anangu culture. Finally, in 2019, a law was passed prohibiting visitors from climbing Uluru. Attempting to climb it is now a breach of the *Environmental Protection and Biodiversity Act 1999* and can result in the imposition of a penalty.

Read the text and answer the following questions.

Who are the traditional owners of Uluru?

____

Why did the traditional owners ask visitors not to climb Uluru?

a) It was against their sacred beliefs.

b) It was too dangerous.

c) It threatened endangered species.

d) It was a breach of the *Environmental Protection and Biodiversity Act*.

All visitors immediately stopped climbing Uluru when the Anangu people asked them to respect their wishes.

True False

Government legislation was needed to enforce the wishes of the Anangu people.

True False

Reflecting on intercultural experiences & taking responsibility

Use words from the word bank to complete the cloze passages.

Word bank

cultural impact democratically

5 **The government listened to the views of the Anangu people and their supporters, showing the importance of acting ________________ when passing laws.**

6 **The Act aims to protect environmental and ______________ values in our society.**

7 **When making laws, the government has to consider the ______________ on people who will be affected by that law.**

Your view

8 **How do you think the Anangu people felt when visitors ignored their wishes and climbed Uluru? What would you have done if you were a visitor?**

____

____

____

____

____

____

____

____

____

____

____

____

____

TARGETING GENERAL CAPABILITIES YEARS 3-4 © PASCAL PRESS ISBN: 9781925726220

Mathematics – Number & Algebra

Australian Curriculum Links: *ACMNA054, ACMNA058, ACMNA077*

Sorry Day Timeline

mid-1800s — The forced removal of Aboriginal and Torres Strait Islander children began.

1909 — The Aborigines Protection Board was granted legal authority to remove Aboriginal children in NSW.

1937 — All states decide to assimilate Aboriginal children of mixed descent (i.e. make them live like white people).

1950s to 1970s — Large numbers of Aboriginal children were taken.

1997 — The *Bringing Them Home* report was released, bringing the issue to national attention.

1998 — The first official Sorry Day was held.

2000 — The Corroboree 2000 Bridge Walk stopped traffic as over 250 000 people walked across the Sydney Harbour Bridge to show support.

2008 — The Prime Minister made an official apology to the Stolen Generations.

Extra facts: The *Bringing Them Home* report found that between one in ten and one in three Aboriginal children were taken from their families as part of the government policy of assimilation.

Source of figures: https://www.reconciliation.org.au/wp-content/uploads/2017/11/150520-Sorry-Day.pdf

Reflecting on intercultural experiences & taking responsibility

Look at the timeline and answer the following questions.

1. How many years passed between the release of the *Bringing Them Home* report and the first official Sorry Day? ______________

2. Write a number sentence to show the difference in time between the year of the report (1997) and the year of the first Sorry Day (1998). Solve the equation. ______________

3. Write a number sentence to show the difference in time between the year in Timeline point 3 and the year in Timeline point 2. Solve the equation. ______________

4. Approximately how many years passed between the start of forced removal and the Prime Minister's formal apology? ______________

5. Write 'one in ten' as a fraction. ______________

6. Write 'one in three' as a fraction. ______________

7. Which fraction is bigger, the answer to Q5 or the answer to Q6? ______________

Your view

8. Which do you feel gives you a better understanding of the Stolen Generations: reading figures about how many children were taken, or hearing the stories of individuals who lived through it? Explain your answer.

____

____

____

____

TARGETING GENERAL CAPABILITIES YEARS 3-4 © PASCAL PRESS ISBN: 9781925726220

Health & Physical Education

Australian Curriculum Links: *ACPPS037, ACPP042*

A stereotype is a belief some people hold about members of a group, based on what they look like. It's a lazy way of thinking. Rather than seeing people as individuals and making an effort to understand them, they only notice external factors, such as their race or culture. This is a form of prejudice—literally 'pre-judging' a person—or making your mind up without knowing anything about them. It can lead to discrimination (treating people differently), hatred, violence and even war.

Many forms of discrimination are illegal in Australia but stereotyping still exists. The best way to challenge prejudices is to 'walk a mile in someone's shoes' or think about what life is like for that person. Getting to know their culture while sharing your own builds trust, respect, and enriches life for everybody.

Read the text and answer the following questions.

What is meant by stereotyping?

a) valuing a person by their appearance rather than their character

b) pre-judging somebody based on external factors

c) giving people a fair go

d) a and b

Which is an example of discrimination?

a) treating someone differently based on their race

b) treating someone differently based on their gender

c) treating someone differently based on their religion

d) all of the above

Reflecting on intercultural experiences & taking responsibility

3 What does it mean to 'walk a mile in someone's shoes'?

4 The Stolen Generations were taken from their families in an attempt to assimilate them, i.e. raise them in the same way as non-Indigenous children. How would you feel if that happened to you?

5 Sorry Day involves taking responsibility and apologising for the Stolen Generations. Do you think it helps make up for some of the pain people experienced? Explain your answer.

6 What does Harmony Week celebrate?

Hint: You can read the passage on page 80.

7 What questions would you ask somebody from another culture in order to learn more about them?

Your turn

8 Imagine your school is planning a day that celebrates diversity and you are asked to contribute something from your own culture to share with others. What would you bring and why?

Self-reflection

This unit was about reflecting on intercultural experiences and taking responsibility. What have you learnt about your own behaviour when it comes to understanding other cultures?

TARGETING GENERAL CAPABILITIES YEARS 3-4 © PASCAL PRESS ISBN: 9781925726220

Recognising culture & developing respect assessment

Investigate culture and cultural identity

This unit talked about the different types of food that cultures enjoy. There are other things that show cultural differences—but there are many more things that show we're all the same, regardless of our heritage.

Use words from the word bank to find things that make different cultures unique and things that are common to everybody in the world. Fill in the table.

Word bank

special foods	friends	love
hopes	traditional music national costumes	family
historical stories	fears	traditional celebrations

Cultural differences	Things we all share

Explore and compare cultural knowledge, beliefs and practices

2 Pick one of the following celebrations: Christmas, Diwali, Eid or Chinese New Year. Describe how families decorate their homes in places where these celebrations are observed.

Develop respect for cultural diversity

3 What is the cultural diversity of your classroom? Ask your classmates to describe the celebrations they enjoy and tell them about your own cultural heritage. Use the space below to write down some of the new things that you have learnt.

TARGETING GENERAL CAPABILITIES YEARS 3-4 © PASCAL PRESS ISBN: 9781925726220

Interacting & empathising with others assessment

Communicate across cultures

This unit talked about creation stories, and in particular the Rainbow Serpent. Stories are one of the things that have defined cultures throughout history. Stories communicate who we are, how we see ourselves, and what we believe in. Stories are told within cultural groups to share a sense of identity. They are also told to people from other groups to aid understanding between cultures. We looked at the different ways in which stories can be told, both in ancient times and today.

1 **Explain what each type means:**

oral storytelling ______________________________

visual storytelling ______________________________

written storytelling ______________________________

2 **What examples were given for each type? Can you add any of your own?**

Oral storytelling examples

____
____
____
____
____

Visual storytelling examples

____
____
____
____
____

Written storytelling examples

Consider and develop multiple perspectives

3 **We talked about the fact that many cultures throughout history have developed creation stories. The stories differ, but they all try to explain how the world came to be. List some other things that different cultures have in common. Remember, they don't have to be identical.**

Empathise with others

Empathy is the ability to understand other people and to share their feelings. It involves being able to imagine what another person is going through, even if we have never been through it ourselves.

4 **Imagine what it would be like to go to school in a country that has a very different culture to your own. Write a diary entry describing how you felt on your first day.**

TARGETING GENERAL CAPABILITIES YEARS 3-4 © PASCAL PRESS ISBN: 9781925726220

Reflecting on intercultural experiences & taking responsibility assessment

Reflect on intercultural experiences

1 **In this unit we looked at the Stolen Generations and the importance of Sorry Day. What has this taught you about the need to understand and respect different cultures?**

____

____

____

____

Challenge stereotypes and prejudices

Often people are judged on what they look like. These are things which people can't control, and they don't tell us anything about what they are really like. This is both unfair and wrong. In order to understand someone, we have to stop generalising and look beyond appearances.

Find words in the word bank that only show what people look like on the outside (external factors) and those that show what they are really like on the inside (internal factors). Fill in the table.

Word bank

friendly smart colouring race brave gender

weight sporty talented height age caring

External factors	Internal factors

Mediate cultural difference

People are encouraged to wear a particular colour during Harmony Day/Week to show their support. Visit https://www.harmony.gov.au/about/ to find out what that colour is and what it represents. Do you have any clothes or accessories of that colour that you can wear? What are they?

ANSWERS

Unit 1

English – Literacy 1 c; 2 a; 3 c; 4 b; 5 d; 6 'Active kids are smarter kids' means that exercise makes both your body and your brain healthier, meaning you will do better in your schoolwork.; 7 They can walk part of the way by walking to a further bus stop or train station than usual, or by driving and parking further away from the school than usual.; 8 Positives examples: walking is free, it doesn't pollute, it's good exercise. Negatives examples: you might live too far away, your bag might be too heavy, it takes longer, it's harder to walk when it's too hot, cold or raining.

Health & Physical Education 1 false; 2 true; 3 true; 4 false; 5 No: cars may be unprepared and unable to stop in time, you might fall over; 6 Jubilee Avenue, Princes Highway; 7 e.g.

8. answers include: to walk with an adult, hold hands, look both ways, listen for traffic, cross at traffic lights or pedestrian crossings, not to run, to pay careful attention

Mathematics – Number and Algebra 1 10; 2

3 2/10; 4 4/10; 5 1/5; 6 1/4; 7 2/8; 8 1/5

Science 1 c; 2 b; 3 d; 4 false; 5 true; 6 true; 7 true; 8 The cars would go further on smooth surfaces such as tiles and floorboards compared to rough surfaces such as carpet.

The Arts – Visual Arts 1 a; 2 c; 3 d; 4 e; 5 b; 6 footpath, hospital, footbridge, police station; 7 swamp, golf course, quarry, cave; 8 Drawings will vary.

Unit 2

English – Literature 1 d; 2 c; 3 a; 4 d; 5 c; 6 A discus is a heavy disk which is thicker in the middle. It can be made of wood or plastic. It is thrown by athletes as part of a sports event, to see who can throw it the furthest.; 7 Greece; 8 Personal responses will vary.

English – Literacy 1 true; 2 false; 3 true; 4 c; 5 a; 6 d; 7 can include: determination, dedication, passion, enthusiastically embracing, smashed it, glittered; 8 Personal responses will vary.

HASS – History 1 d; 2 b; 3 a; 4 c; 5 false; 6 true; 7 false; 8 Personal responses will vary.

Technologies – Digital Technologies 1 a; 2 d; 3 d; 4 true; 5 true; 6 false; 7 delete the comments, delete the entire post, seek help from a parent or teacher, block the people who made the rude comments, consider reporting them; 8 may include: unflattering or ugly photographs, rude comments, images of people falling over, images of people crying, identifying information

Health & Physical Education 1 Doctors discovered he had a rare liver condition and was therefore unable to do contact sport.; 2 Harradine took up field athletics instead.; 3 His motivation slipped because he wasn't happy with his performance.; 4 He started wearing colourful sports clothes to bring back the joy. It worked because it reminded him to enjoy the process, rather than focus on the results.; 5 family; 6 optimists; 7 early; 8 succeed

Unit 3

English – Language 1 a; 2 b; 3 d; 4 c; 5 true; 6 false; 7 true; 8 Personal responses will vary.

English – Literature 1 c; 2 d; 3 true; 4 true; 5 false; 6 to show they oppose the building of the highway; 7 crime, gouging, harming; 8 Personal responses will vary.

HASS – Geography 1 true; 2 false; 3 false; 4 true; 5 It adds nutrients to the soil and makes room for new plants to grow.; 6 It would reduce the amount of fuel the fire could burn.; 7 It means we can learn from traditional techniques and use some of them alongside our existing efforts.; 8 That she should talk to the Ngarigo elders and learn how their traditional methods can be used to help prevent devastating bushfires today.

HASS – Civics and Citizenship 1 b; 2 d; 3 false; 4 true; 5 true; 6 false; 7 Monaro Residents' Committee members, elders of the Ngarigo people, environmental activists; 8 It would still be worth it as it gives people an opportunity to discuss alternative plans and options, and local roads would need to connect to the highway anyway.

Health & Physical Education 1 true; 2 true; 3 false; 4 true; 5 false; 6 It may be a form of bullying because refusing to let people have a say can make them feel unvalued. Bullying behaviour can take many forms, not just physical; 7 & 8 Personal responses will vary.

Unit 4

English – Language 1 d; 2 b; 3 a; 4 c; 5 new, illness, contagious; 6 vulnerable, threat, risk; 7 lucky, safely, beat; 8 Personal responses will vary.

HASS – Civics and Citizenship 1 true; 2 false; 3 false; 4 d; 5 Wear school hat outdoors. No bombing in the pool. Eat dinner before dessert. 6 Don't speed while driving. Don't go through red lights. No trespassing. 7 d; 8 Personal responses will vary.

Mathematics – Statistics and Probablilty 1 c; 2 a; 3 b; 4 b; 5 elbows; 6 open air; 7 answer = elbows – hands i.e. 12-6=6; 8 answers depend on class survey

TARGETING GENERAL CAPABILITIES YEARS 3-4 © PASCAL PRESS ISBN: 9781925726220

Technologies Digital 1 true; 2 true; 3 true; 4 true; 5 false; 6 The answers could have been anonymous.; 7 Rachel should have asked her classmates' permission and/or not used identifying information.; 8 Rachel's action are not really justified as it caused Leo much distress and lead to conflict in their class. A better way to have encouraged him to perform good hand hygiene would have been to educate him as to the risks of his actions.

PERSONAL AND SOCIAL CAPABILITY ASSESSMENT

Answers are not provided for tasks where personal responses will vary.

Self-awareness

6

Seeing learners	*Hearing learners*	*Writing learners*	*Doing learners*
Look at diagrams	Listen to teacher	Read book	Follow demonstration
Look at infographics	Listen to podcast	Write notes	Perform experiment

Self-management

1 She probably didn't win because she is looking sad and disappointed.

3 Possible answers include: encourage her not to give up, tell her to try again, say she'll do better next time, remind her that she still had fun trying etc., suggest she set up a schedule for practice and set smaller goals that lead up to bigger ones.

4 Keep trying, be positive, ask for help, take a chance, learn more, enjoy the process.

Social awareness

1

Who?	What do they want?	Why?
Monaro Residents' Association	To build a new road	To allow access to safety during a bushfire
The Ngarigo people	The new road to be moved	To prevent it harming sacred land
Environmental activists	No new road to be built	Building roads harms the environment

ANSWERS

5

Positive effect	Negative effect
discussing	ignoring
listening	sarcasm
patience	interrupting
taking turns	shouting
applauding	booing

Social management

2 The government would have considered how easy it is to catch the disease, how deadly it is, how long it would take to develop a vaccine and treatment, what the effect would be on the economy, and what the effect would be on people's mental health.

3 i explain; ii talk; iii listen; iv respect; v most

4 Answers may include: invasions, wars, major natural disasters, major industrial accidents, major economic crises.

INTERCULTURAL UNDERSTANDING

Unit 5

English – Language 1 b; 2 b; 3 a 4 A topic sentence opens a paragraph and predicts how the paragraph will develop. Students can choose the first sentence of any paragraph.; 5 contractions, informal; 6 Greek, basil pie; 7 c; 8 Personal responses may vary but are likely to include the British Christmas pudding tradition.

HASS – History 1 false; 2 true; 3 b; 4 b; 5 d; 6 We have a large Chinese population in Australia, and they share their culture and history; 7 Both involve spending time with family, both involve gifts of money, both traditions are followed in Australia; 8 personal responses will vary.

HASS – Geography 1 New Zealand; 2 Indonesia; 3 Papua New Guinea; 4 More crowded because there are more people in less space.; 5 Maori; 6 true; 7 true; 8 Personal responses will vary.

Technologies – Design and Technology 1 d; 2 c; 3 a; 4 true; 5 false; 6 WA, SA, Vic, Tas, NSW, Qld; 7 Modern societies like Australia, as modern methods allow for mass production.; 8 Personal responses will vary, and the soft, fine texture of white flour is more suitable for making sweet breads and cakes.

Health & Physical Education 1 gulab jamun India, vasilopita Greece, baklava Middle East, mooncake China, Christmas pudding UK; 2 Christmas; 3 New Year; 4 Eid; 5 Mid-autumn Festival; 6 Diwali; 7 and 8 Personal responses will vary.

TARGETING GENERAL CAPABILITIES YEARS 3-4 © PASCAL PRESS ISBN: 9781925726220

Unit 6

English – Language 1 Stories that try to explain how the world was made and why it is the way that it is.; 2 The acts of creation according to Australians Aboriginal creation stories; 3 true; 4 false; 5 c; 6 There are different names for the Rainbow Serpent because there are many different Indigenous language groups. This is because Australia is very large and the different language groups are scattered across the country.; 7

oral	visual	written
song	dance	poem
recital	artwork	novel
audiobook	movie	script

8 Personal responses will vary.

HASS – History 1 at least 40 000 years; 2 false; 3 true; 4 true; 5 A dialect is a different form of a language that developed over time to suit a particular environment or culture.; 6 d; 7 Torres Strait Islanders; 8 Personal responses will vary.

HASS – Geography 1 Qld, NSW, ACT, Vic, Tas, SA, WA, NT; 2 different language groups and nations; 3 false; 4 true; 5 coasts; 6 adapted; 7 landscapes; 8 Personal responses will vary.

The Arts – Visual Arts 1 d; 2 c; 3 a; 4 true; 5 false; 6 Personal responses will vary.; 7 They weren't meant to be admired purely as an artwork, but held deep spiritual meanings that non-Indigenous people may not be aware of.

The Arts – Dance 1 true; 2 false; 3 true; 4 space, time, dynamics, relationships; 5 They are keeping low to the ground, which might suggest their connection to the land.; 6 strong, rhythmic movements; 7 The four dancers are in a close group, all facing in the same direction. They have similar stances but different heights and arm gestures.; 8 Personal responses will vary.

Unit 7

English – Language 1 d; 2 c; 3 a; 4 true; 5 false; 6 Rudd repeatedly uses 'we' to refer to all Australians, e.g. 'we apologise' 'we are sorry'.; 7 factual reporting; 8 Personal responses will vary.

HASS – History 1 b; 2 c; 3 b; 4 true; 5 false; 6 It took many years for the nation to recognise the importance of the Indigenous population and to understand the nature of the atrocities that had been committed against them.; 7 All three flags are flown to symbolise the unity between all Indigenous and non-Indigenous Australians, as a way of reconciling and healing rifts.; 8 Personal responses will vary.

HASS – Civics and Citizenship 1 the Anangu people; 2 a; 3 false; 4 true; 5 democratically; 6 cultural; 7 impact; 8 Personal responses will vary.

Mathematics – Number and Algebra 1 one year; 1998 – 1997 = 1; 3 1937 – 1909 = 28; 4 approximately 150 years; 5 1/10; 6 1/3; 7 the answer to Q6 i.e. 1/3; 8 Personal responses will vary.

Health & Physical Education 1 d; 2 d; 3 It means to try to imagine what life is like to that person.; 4 & 5 Personal responses will vary.; 6 Harmony Week celebrates all the nationalities that make up Australia, and it allows people to learn about other cultures.; 7 & 8 Personal responses will vary.

INTERCULTURAL UNDERSTANDING ASSESSMENT

Answers are not provided for tasks where personal responses will vary.

Recognising culture & developing respect

1

Cultural differences	Things we all share
special foods	hopes
historical stories	fears
traditional music	love
national costumes	family
traditional celebrations	friends

2 Answers can include but are not limited to: Christmas – decorated trees, lights, stockings, nativity scenes, Santas; Diwali – lampshades, candles, lanterns, Rangoli; Eid – lanterns, balloons, star and moon decorations; Chinese New Year – red lanterns, paper cuttings, doorway banners, paintings.

Interacting & empathising with others

1 Oral storytelling refers to a tradition where stories are shared, often across generations, by being told and retold. Visual storytelling means that stories are presented in the form of visual images. Written storytelling means that the stories are written down in words.

2 Oral examples: recitals, songs, audiobooks; Visual examples: movies, artwork (paintings, sculptures, etc.), television shows; Written examples: novels, poetry, scripts, non-fiction books.

3 Answers can include music, festivals, celebrations, clothing, national costumes, foods, sport, games, myths and legends, religions and religious beliefs.

Reflecting on intercultural experiences & taking responsibility

2

External factors	Internal factors
colouring	friendly
race	smart
gender	brave
weight	sporty
height	talented
age	caring

3 The colour chosen to represent Harmony Week is orange. It represents communication, the freedom of ideas and mutual respect.

Targeting: General Capabilities
Personal & Social Capability and Intercultural Understanding Years 3-4

ISBN: 9781925726220

Published by Pascal Press
PO Box 250
Glebe NSW 2037
www.pascalpress.com.au

contact@pascalpress.com.au

Author: Stella Tarakson
Publisher: Lynn Dickinson
Typesetter: Stacey Grainger
Editor: Marie Theodore

Printed in South Korea by Prinpia Co., Ltd.

CONTENTS

HOW TO USE THIS BOOK

General Capabilities form one dimension of the Australian Curriculum, the others being the Learning Areas and the Cross-Curriculum Priorities. General Capabilities are taught through the content of the Learning Areas and involve knowledge, skills, behaviour and dispositions.

There are seven General Capabilities, and this Targeting General Capabilities book examines two of them: Personal and Social Capability, and Intercultural Understanding. The two General Capabilities are further divided into their elements: seven in all. Each unit begins with a stimulus, followed by assessable activities that examine the element through the different Learning Areas. The table below provides a quick page reference to the different Learning Areas examined via each General Capability element in this book. You will find the relevant links to the Australian Curriculum at the beginning of each section.

Unit	Elements	English	HASS	HPE	Maths	Science	Tech	The Arts
	Personal & Social Capability							
1	Self- awareness	6	12	14	8, 10			
2	Self-management	17	20	27		23	25	
3	Social awareness	30	32	38	36	34		
4	Social management	41	43, 45				47, 49	
	Intercultural Understanding							
5	Recognising culture	61	63, 65	69				67
6	Interacting & empathising	72	74, 76			78	80	
7	Reflecting & taking responsibility	83	85, 87	89				91

On the last page of each unit, space is allocated for self-reflection. Students have the opportunity to explore what they have learnt about each element and to record their thoughts.

There is an assessment section at the end of each General Capability element where tasks are tailored to the sub-elements, rather than through the lens of a specific Learning Area. This consolidates students' understanding of the concepts and provides guidance for further reflection.

Personal & Social Capability

Personal and Social Capability encourages children to be aware of their emotions and learn how to manage their feelings, behaviours and interactions with others. As outlined in the curriculum, the elements and sub-elements are:

 **Self-awareness** — recognise emotions; recognise personal qualities and achievements; understand themselves as learners; develop reflective practice

 **Self-management** — express emotions appropriately; develop self-discipline and set goals; work independently and show initiative; become confident, resilient and adaptable

 **Social awareness** — appreciate diverse perspectives; contribute to civil society; understand relationships

 **Social management** — communicate effectively; work collaboratively; make decisions, negotiate and resolve conflict; develop leadership skills.

Self-awareness

What is a fad? When someone refers to a 'fad', they usually mean something that a group of people gets very excited about for a short amount of time. This can be an interest, a toy, or even a type of dance or fashion. Some fads become popular again after a long time as a new generation discovers them. People often look back at fads fondly when they think about the fun they had at the time, even though they may not be excited about the fad anymore.

Wheeled fads

Devices with wheels have been a favourite with kids of all ages for a very long time. Back in the 1950s and 1960s, children often built their own go-karts to race each other. In the 1970s, people enjoyed rollerskating at roller discos, where they played disco music while people skated around a rink. In the 1980s and 1990s, colourful inline skates known as Rollerblades became popular. Today, it's very common to see kids riding down the street on the latest scooters and skateboards. Rollerskates have made a comeback in the past few years, as they are used in the competitive sport known as roller derby.

TARGETING GENERAL CAPABILITIES YEARS 5-6 © PASCAL PRESS ISBN: 9781925726237